AWS CERTIFIED SOLUTION ARCHITECT ASSOCIATE

The Complete Guide To The Ssa-C02 Exam, Traning To Expand
Your Knowledge Before Exams, Useful Tips On How To Start
Your New Career & Approach A New Job

DERICK CARTER

TABLE OF CONTENTS

Introduction

Amazon Web Services may seem like a technical buzzword, but there is more to it than just the name. From booking flights and hotels on Expedia to binge-watching my favorite seasons on Netflix to buying products on Amazon. All has been made possible—Thanks to Amazon Web Services, which plays a pivotal role in assisting renowned companies spread across different parts of the world, such as Europe, the USA, and Asia. By 2014, AWS had a hold of 1.4 million servers and emerged as a strong competitor in the cloud computing platform.

The AWS not only provides hardware and computing resources but also renders Software functionalities. For over 9 consecutive years, The IT firm Gartner has declared AWS as a leader in Magic Quadrant for Cloud Infrastructure, proving how flexible and robust the technology is.

What Is Amazon Web Services?
The Origin

In the olden days, the companies had their own data centers where they had hardware resources, computers, and professional IT teams to manage the entire system, which meant that plenty of time and effort was required into the computer systems.

As a greater number of hardware types of equipment increased, the processing power also increased, resulting in higher power consumption that could put the entire system at risk. Most companies and entrepreneurs didn't have enough money to invest in the infrastructure of their own, which became a barrier for companies to flourish in their respective targets.

Early in the '90s, Amazon came up with a revolutionary solution to solve the underlying problem. The Amazon CEO, Jeff Bezos, put forward the idea of establishing data centers equipped with hardware resources, storage, and sufficient power so that other companies can utilize it instead of building their own data centers, which can definitely cost a fortune.

Instead of building an infrastructure from scratch, organizations can simply use the data centers provided by AWS on rent, allowing them to progress. This means that companies don't have to build their infrastructure when they can use reliable and powerful technology offered by Amazon. The data centers are widely spread across the globe. If one center fails, it's easy to shift over to the data center present in another location.

What Are the Uses of AWS?

AWS provides a list of services that includes hosting websites, storing data into databases, game development, IoT, and Artificial Intelligence.

Based on the company's needs, I choose a handful of services I require. These services are collectively known as cloud computing. With cloud computing, large-scale businesses no longer have to purchase and set up IT infrastructure for months. Instead, the servers can roll over in minutes using AWS.

AWS aims to provide scalable, fast, and affordable services in around 190 countries.

What Is Cloud Computing?

Cloud Computing is a technical term for providing and using IT resources needed by any business. The resources range from power, storage, applications, and many more that can be accessed through the internet with the pay-as-you-go pricing.

Whether I wish to store huge amounts of data or support my IT department, Cloud computing enables access to various affordable IT resources. I don't have to spend huge amounts of money on building up the hardware infrastructure. Instead, I can choose the number of resources I need, the size of the equipment, and the power I require. Moreover, I can have access to as many equipments and pay accordingly, no matter where I am.

Through a cloud services platform, I can gain access to databases, servers, storage, and a set of application services easily using the World Wide Web. The AWS is a highly flexible and reliable cloud computing platform that is responsible for managing the hardware resources. The resources aren't noticeable to the user as the cloud platform offers a degree of abstraction, which may differ from virtual hardware to complex systems.

CHAPTER 1:

The New SAA-C02 Exam Version

The New Version of the SAA-C02 Exam

The new SAA-C02 exam for the AWS Certified Solutions Architect Associate certification is available as of March 2020. The previous form of the exam was retired on July 1, 2020, after being extended for a few more months due to the closure of screening tests caused by the COVID-19 pandemic. It has been updated with new content to align with the latest AWS features and services.

To help you better prepare for the exam, let's take a look at the exam design and break down the different "domains" in the exam guide so you know what to expect.

Understand the AWS Exam Design

This exam qualifies for membership in the AWS training program and is recommended for people with at least one year of practical experience. The exam is for solution architects and requires you to demonstrate knowledge of how to define a solution using architectural design principles based on customer requirements and provide best practice-based implementation guidance for the organization throughout the lifecycle. The "AWS Certified Solutions Architect Associate Exam Guide (SAA-C02)" recommends the following AWS skills:

- One year of hands-on experience designing scalable, fault-tolerant, accessible distributed systems available on AWS.

- Hands-on experience with AWS computer, networking, storage, and database services.

- Hands-on experience with AWS distribution and management services.

- Knowledge of the best practices recommended to create secure and reliable applications on the AWS platform.

- Understand the basic principles of the AWS cloud authoring architecture.

- Understanding of the global AWS infrastructure.

- Understanding of network technologies in relation to AWS.

- Understand the security features and tools provided by AWS and their relationship to traditional service.

The exam includes 65 questions and has a time limit of 130 minutes. You must obtain a minimum score of 720 points out of 1000 to pass the exam.

The exam question format is one of the following:

- Multiple choice (one correct answer of four choices)

- Multiple choice (two or more correct answers of five or more choices)

- Most questions are 1 to 2 lines of a scenario, followed by the question itself.

Important: Be very careful when reading the question text to make sure you select the correct answer! Sometimes it's easy to miss small details that change your answer, so don't rush your pass.

AWS SAA-CO2 Exam Question Allocation Table Content Outline

The exam has the following content domains that each make up a percentage of the exam:

Domain 1: Design Resilient Architectures, which makes up 30% of the exams.

This domain consists of the following topics or concepts for resilient AWS architectures:

Domain 2: Design High-Performing Architectures which make up 28% of the exams.

This domain consists of the following topics or concepts pertaining to a workload:

- Identify scalable and elastic compute solutions for a workload.

- Select scalable and high-performing storage solutions for a workload.

- Select networking solutions based on high-performance for a workload.

- Select database solutions for a workload that are high-performance.

Domain 3: Design Secure Applications and Architectures, which make up 24% of the exams. This domain consists of the following topics or concepts about security:

- The learner must be able to design secure access to AWS resources.

- The learners must understand and be able to design secure application tiers.

- The learner must be confident enough to select appropriate data security options.

Domain 4: Design Cost-Optimized Architectures which make up 18% of the exams.

This domain consists of the following topics or concepts about cost-optimization of AWS:

- This domain requires the student to be able to identify cost-effective storage solutions.

- The student must know how to identify database services and compute cost-effective services.

- The student must be able to design cost-effective network architectures expertly.

What to Expect From the Exam

To do well and pass the exam, the student is expected to know the AWS core services and how to use them to create systems that follow AWS best practices.

Every missed answer is marked as an incorrect answer, and an incorrect answer will bring down the overall score of the exam.

A question can be marked for future consideration, but try and guess what you think it may be before moving on to the next question. That way, if time runs out and you have not had a chance to go back to review the question, you have a chance of getting it right as opposed to not answering it at all.

At the end of the exam, you can review each answer and questions you have marked for review. Marking a question for review also makes it easier to get back to, especially when time is running short.

It is important to keep an eye on the time periodically throughout the exam, and if you feel you are spending too much time on a question, mark it for review rather than keep going back to it.

The exam content will contain questions that are broken down into **Response Types** and **Unscored Content**.

When taking the exams, it is vital to remember that all the details on the test questions may count.

Response Types

The examination is broken down into two types of questions that will be asked of the student. These questions are:

• **Multiple choice questions**—These questions only have one correct answer, but the student will be given a choice of four answers to choose from. The three incorrect answers are what are known as **distractor** answers.

Example:

Q1: What is the color of the sky?

    A. Orange

    B. Green

    C. Azure

    D. Lemon

Answer: C. Azure

• **Multiple response questions**—These types usually have one question with 5 to 6 answers to choose from. It will be stated how many correct answers to choose from the list of given answers. For instance, the question may say something like, from the following list, choose the two correct answers. Example:

Q2: What are the parts of a motor car?

Choose two.

    A. Seat

    B. Jar

    C. Engine

    D. Lid

    E. Bag

Answer: A. Seat & C. Engine

Not all of the questions will be ones that have obvious answers that stand out. Some of the questions will require the exam taker to choose the right procedure or solution for the scenario put forward in the matter. Example:

Q3: Mary needs to make some toast with butter and jam. From the options below, choose the procedure that explains how to best make the buttered toast.

    A. Put the bread on the plate and butter it with fresh butter.

    B. Put the butter and bread on the plate with a knife.

    C. Put the bread and butter in the oven on high for 20 minutes.

    D. Put the bread in the toaster, and when it pops out, put it on a plate and butter the bread.

Answer: D. Put the bread in the toaster and when it pops out, put it on a plate and butter the bread.

Work through the questions by eliminating answers that you are sure do not pertain to the question. If you know the subject well enough, the incorrect answers will be clearer. There are always two answers that will look pretty similar. They need to be read through really carefully because this is what trips a student up.

Unscored Content

There may be what is called unscored content included on the exam. Although they do not affect the exam taker's score, they are there to gather statistical information.

End of the Exam

It is a good idea to flag questions you had doubts about, so if you have time at the end of the exam, you can review them.

At the end of the exam, the student will receive their mark and whether or not they passed the exam. They will also get the statistics on what their strengths and weaknesses were for the subject based on answers.

Whether the student passes or fails the exam, the strength and weakness table is a valuable tool. It will show the learner what they need to work on within the AWS domain to continue focusing on.

Do not let it discourage you if you did not pass the first time around, not many people do. But you will know what you need to go back and work on to ensure you do pass the next time around.

CHAPTER 2:

Elastic Compute Cloud (Ec2)

A WS EC2 provides an IaaS product. The computing is done on AWS using Amazon EC2. These are virtual servers called instances with high computing power. It provides an automatic resizing tool to change capacity dynamically. EC2 container registry and EC2 allow clients to work with containers and Docker images on the AWS platform.

EC2 is also helpful for server hosting and setup process. With Amazon EC2, it becomes very easy to distribute your server. The EC2 is a powerful web service that is secure, customizable with high computing capacity in the cloud. This simple web services interface permits you to acquire and develop capacity with a nominal force. Get full control of IT assets, and you can work in the IT environment configured by Amazon.

Virtualization

The servers are configured in three sections without virtualization:

• CPU hardware

• Core

Operating system

It works in privileged mode and can directly interact with the hardware.

• User mode

Run applications.

You can make a system call to the kernel to interact with the hardware.

If an application tries to interact with the hardware without a system call, it will cause a system error and may crash the server or at least the application.

Emulated Virtualization: Software Virtualization

The host operating system was running on HW and included a hypervisor (HV). SW worked in privileged mode and had full access to HW. Guest operating system wrapped in a virtual machine and with devices mapped to your operating system to emulate real hardware. Drivers, like graphics cards, have been emulated SW to allow the process to work properly.

The guest operating system still believed it was running on real HW and attempted to take control of HW. The areas were not real, and at the moment, they were only given a space.

The HV performs the binary translation. Along the way, system calls are intercepted and translated to SW. The guest operating system does not need changes, but it slows down a lot.

Paravirtualization

The guest operating system is modified and runs in HV containers, except that it does not use slow binary translation.

The operating system is changed to change system calls to user calls. Instead of calling HW, they call HV using hyper call. The areas of the operating system call HV instead of HW.

Hardware-Assisted Virtualization

The physical hardware itself is aware of virtualization. The CPU has specific functions for the HV to enter and support.

When the guest operating system tries to execute privileged instructions, they are trapped by the CPU and do not stop the process. They are redirected to HV by HW.

What matters for a VM is inbound and outbound operations, such as network transfer and IO disk. The problem is that multiple operating systems try to access the same hardware component, but are involved in sharing.

SR-IOV (Singe Route IO Virtualization)

It allows a network or any card to resemble many mini cards. As for the HW, they are truly dedicated cards for your use. The HV should not do any translation.

The physical card handles everything. In EC2, this feature is called an enhanced network.

EC2 Architecture and Resilience

EC2 instances are virtual machines running on EC2 hosts.

Tenancy:

• Shared: Instances run on shared hardware but isolated from other clients.

• Dedicated: Instances run on hardware dedicated to a single client. Dedicated instances can share hardware with other instances of the same AWS account that are not dedicated instances.

• Dedicated Host: Instances run on a fully dedicated physical server for your use. Pay for the entire host, don't pay for instances.

• Tough AZ service. They operate within a single AZ system. It cannot be accessed through the area.

EC2 host contains:

• Local hardware like CPU and memory

• They also have a temporary app store.

    If the instance moves the hosts, memory is lost.

• You can use remote archiving, Elastic Block Store (EBS).

    EBS allows you to assign persistent storage volumes to instances within AZ itself.

• Two types of networks

    Storage network

    Data network.

ENI—EC2 Network

When provisioning instances within a specific subnet within a VPC, a primary elastic network interface is provided on a subnet that joins the physical hardware on the EC2 host. Subnets are also within a specific AZ. These Instances can have numerous network interfaces, even within different subnets, as long as they are on the same AZ. An instance is running on a specific host. If you restart the instance, it will remain on that host until:

• Host fails or is removed from AWS

• The instance stops and then starts, other than the restarted one.

The instance will be transferred to another host in the same AZ. Instances cannot be moved to different AZs. Everything related to your hardware is stuck within an AZ specification.

A migration is acquiring a copy of an instance and moving it to another AZ. In general cases of the same type and generation, it will occupy the same host. The only difference will generally be its size.

EC2 Strengths

Durable calculation needs. Many other AWS services have runtime limits.

• Server-style applications

• Things waiting for the network response

• Explosion or constant charge

• Monolithic application stack

Middleware or specific runtime components

• Application workload migration or disaster recovery

To intervene in the existing applications running on a server and backup system.

EC2 Instance Types

• General Purpose (T, M): Predefined steady-state workloads with uniform resources

• Optimized calculation (C): media processing, scientific modeling, and games

• Optimized memory (R, X): processing large data sets in memory

• Accelerated Processing (P, G, F): Hardware GPU, FPGA

• Optimized Storage (H, I, D)—Large amounts of super-fast local memory. Huge amounts of IO per second. Elastic research and analytical workloads.

Naming scheme

R5dn.8xlarge—Everything is the instance type. If in doubt, provide the full instance type

• 1st character: A family of instances.

• 2nd character: generation of the instance. In general, always select the latest generation.

• Character after the period: instance size. CPU and memory considerations.

Often a simpler sizing system with a larger number of smaller instance sizes.

• 3rd period—previous period: additional features

    A: AMD CPU

    D: NVMe memory

    N: Optimized network

    E: Additional capacity for ram or storage.

Storage Refresher

Instance Store

• Directly connected memory (local)

• Super-fast

• Temporary or temporary memory.

Elastic Block Store (EBS)

• Network storage

• Volumes delivered on the network

• Persistent archiving survives beyond the duration of the instance.

Three Types of Storage

• **Block storage:** volume presented to the operating system as a collection of blocks. No structure beyond that. These are mountable and startable. The operating system will create a file system in addition to this, NTFS or EXT3, and then mount it as a root or volume drive in Linux. Rotation of hard drives or SSDs. This could also be provided by a physical volume. It does not have an integrated structure.

You can mount an EBS volume or start an EBS volume.

• **File storage:** displayed as a file share with a structure. You can access files through memory. You cannot boot from memory, but you can mount it.

• **Archive objects:** A flat collection of objects. The object can be anything with or without associated metadata. To retrieve the object, the key must be supplied, and the value will be returned. This cannot be mounted or started. It is very well resized and can have simultaneous access.

Storage Performance

• IO Block Size: Determines how to split the data.

• IOPS: How many reads or writes can a system contain per second.

• Effective speed: final frequency reached, expressed in MB/s (megabytes per second).

Block size * IOPS = Performance

This is not the only part of the chain, but it is a simplification. A system may have an effective speed limit. IOPS may decrease with increasing block size.

_EBS—Elastic Block Store

• Assign block storage volumes to instances.

• The volumes are isolated in an AZ.

The data is highly available and robust for that AZ.

All data is replicated in that AZ. All AZ must have a big flaw to get out.

• There are two types of physical storage (SSD/HDD)

• Variable performance level (IOPS, T-put)

• Billed as GB/month.

> If you provide 1 TB for a full month, you will be charged as such.

> If you have half the data, you will be charged half the month.

• There are four types of volumes, each with a dominant performance attribute.

> Generic SSD (gp2)

> IOPS SSO with provisioning (io1)

▪ Maximum IOPS as database

> T-put HDD optimized (st1)

▪ Maximum T-put for records or multimedia storage

> Cold HDD (sc1)

EBS Exam Power-Ups

• Volumes are generated in an AZ, isolated in AZ.

• If an AZ fails, the volume is affected.

• Highly available and rugged in that AZ. The only reason for failure is if all AZ fails.

• Usually from a volume to an instance, except io1 with multiple connections

- It has a speed of GB/m regardless of the state of the instance.

- Maximum EBS at 80k IOPS per instance and 64k vol (io1)

- 1000 MiB/s (vol) (io1), Max. 2375 MB/s per instance

EC2 Instance Store

- Local block memory attached to an instance.

- Physically connected to an EC2 host.

> They are isolated for that specific host.

> Instances on that host can access them.

- Maximum storage performance on AWS.

- Included in the price of the instance, use it or lose it.

- It can ONLY be connected at startup.

Summary

The base programming stack that sudden spikes in demand for an EC2 case are characterized by your decision of Amazon Machine Image and any contents or client information you include at dispatch time and the equipment profile is the result of an occurrence type. A tenure setting decides if your case will impart a physical host to different cases.

Similarly, as with all your AWS assets, it's critical to give your EC2 occurrences effectively recognizable labels that adjust to a framework wide naming show. There are points of confinement to the amount of assets you'll be permitted to dispatch inside a solitary district and record wide. Should you hit your cutoff, you can generally demand access to extra assets.

In the event that you intend to run an occasion for a year or more, you can spare a lot of cash overpaying for on-request by obtaining a held example. If your remaining task at hand can withstand unforeseen shutdowns, at that point, a spot occurrence could likewise bode well.

There are four sorts of Elastic Block Store volumes: two high IOPS and low-inactivity SSD types and two conventional hard drives. Your remaining burden and spending will advise your decision. Likewise, some EC2 example types accompany transient case store volumes that offer quick information get to, however, whose information is lost when the occurrence is closed down.

Exercise

Launch an EC2 Linux instance and login using SSh.

1. On the Configure Security Group page, make sure there's a rule permitting incoming SSH (port 22) traffic. It should be there by default.

2. Before letting you launch the instance, AWS will require you to select—or create—a key pair. Follow the instructions.

3. Once the instance is launched, you can return to the Instances Dashboard to wait until everything is running properly.

4. Click the Actions pull-down and then the Connect item for instructions on how to connect to the instance from your local machine. Then connect and take a look at your virtual cloud server.

CHAPTER 3:

Elastic Load Balancing and Auto Scaling

Elastic Load Balancing

LB or Elastic load balancing helps in automatic distribution of the traffics of an application across various targets such as containers, instances of Amazon EC2, Lambda functions, and IP addresses. ELB can easily cope up with the fluctuating traffic application load across multiple or in a single AZ. Elastic load balancing or ELB comes with three different load balancers, which features automatic scaling, high availability along with robust security, that is very much necessary for making the applications tolerant of all kinds of faults.

- **Application Load Balancer:** This load balancer type is the best option for load balancing for HTTPS and HTTP traffic. It helps with an advanced type of request routing, which is targeted to the very delivery of the architectures of modern applications that also includes containers and microservices. This load balancer works at the individual layer of request and routes traffic within the Amazon VPC, which is based on the requested content.

- **Network Load Balancer:** This load balancer type is the best option for TCP or Transmission Control Protocol load balancing, TLS or Transport Layer Security, and UDP or User Datagram Protocol where high-end performance is required. It operates at the level of connection and routes the traffic to several types of targets in the VPC. It has the capacity of easily handling a huge number of user requests every second along with maintenance of super-low latencies side by side. The network load balancer is optimized in a way so that it can also handle volatile and sudden patterns of traffic.

- **Classic Load Balancer:** This type of load balancer provides load balancing at the basic level across various instances of Amazon EC2. It operates both at the connection level and at the request level. This type of load balancer is best for those types of applications, which are built within the classic EC2 network.

Benefits of ELB or Elastic Load Balancing

ELB comes with various benefits for the users:

High availability

Along with the distribution of traffic across several targets, ELB also loads balance across the region by routing traffic to the healthy targets in various availability zones. The Amazon ELB commits for 99.99% of availability for a load balancer.

Secure

ELB or Elastic Load Balancing works hand in hand with Amazon VPC for providing potent features of security that also includes authentication of the user, integrated management of certificate, and SSL/TLS decryption. By combing all of these, ELB provides you with the ultimate flexibility for managing the settings of TLS and offload the CPU workload from the applications.

Elastic

ELB can easily handle sudden and rapid changes in the patterns of network traffic. Additionally, Auto Scaling with deep integration makes sure of up to the marked capacity of the applications for meeting the varying application loads without the requirement of manual intervention.

Flexibility

Elastic Load Balancing or ELB allows users to use their IP addresses for routing the requests to the application targets. This, in turn, provides you with flexibility in the way you are going to virtualize the application targets and thus allows you to host more than one application on a similar instance. This also allows the applications to enjoy their security groups, respectively, and use a parallel port of network for further simplification of the inter-application communication in an architecture based on microservice.

Potent Auditing and Monitoring

ELB allows the users to monitor their applications along with their performances in real-time with the use of Amazon CloudWatch, logging, and metrics and tracing of requests. This helps in improving the overall visibility of your application behavior, identify the bottlenecks of performance, and uncover the issues of your application stack on an individual request.

Hybrid Balancing of Load

Elastic Load Balancing offers the ability to balance the load for AWS along with on-premises source by using the same balancer of the load. This makes it easier for the users to migrate, failover, or bursts the on-premises applications available on the cloud.

Features

Achieving a better level of fault tolerance for the applications

ELB provides an easy level of fault tolerance, which is required for the applications by automatic balancing all the network traffic to the available targets. In case not all the targets in the availability zone are healthy, ELB routes the traffic to the other health targets in another availability zone. Once the targets in the availability zone return to a healthy state, the load balancing automatically returns to the original targets.

Automated scaling of applications

ELB provides the users with the confidence that the application will effectively scale to the customer demands. With the feature of Auto Scaling for the instances of Amazon EC2 when the latency of any of the instances exceeds the threshold that was preconfigured, the application will be ready for serving the next request of the customer.

ELB and VPC

ELB makes the creation of an internet entry point into the user's VPC an easy job. You can seamlessly assign the security groups to the load balancer for controlling which of the ports are in the open state for the allowed sources.

As ELB comes integrated with the VPC, all the existing ACLs or Network Access Control Lists continue providing additional control of the network.

When you create a load balancer for your dedicated VPC, you can choose whether the load balancer will be internal or internet-facing which is by default. In case you choose internally, you do not need to have an internet gateway for reaching out to the load balancer. The private IP address that comes with a load balancer will be used for the DNS record of the load balancer.

The user can configure the checking of the health of your targets so that the ELB is capable of request sending to healthy targets only. You can offload the overall work of encryption and decryption to the ELB for making the resources of computing to focus on the main job.

Auto-Scaling

The AWS Auto-scaling helps in monitoring the applications and automatically adjusts the capacity for maintaining predictable and steady performance and that too at a reasonable price. The auto-scaling comes with the easy setup process for scaling the applications for various resources beyond numerous services within a minute. The auto-scaling service provides a very powerful and simple interface for the users that will help you a lot in planning the plans of scaling of the resources that also include Spot Fleets and instances of Amazon EC2, Amazon DynamoDB indexes, and tables, Amazon ECS tasks along with Amazon Aurora Replicas.

The service of Auto Scaling from AWS makes the step of scaling a simple job along with various recommendations, which will allow optimization of the overall costs, performance, and perfect balance between all. It also helps in maintaining the availability of the applications and allows the users to remove or add instances of EC2 according to the defined conditions.

The dynamic scaling system responds automatically to the change in the demands and the system of predictive scaling schedules a perfect number of instances of EC2, which is established on the demand that is being predicted.

Benefits of Auto-Scaling

The EC2 auto-scaling comes with various features that can help you in improving the overall functioning of your applications.

- **Improvement of fault tolerance:** The system of auto-scaling can easily detect when the EC2 instance is in an unhealthy condition, terminates the same, and replaces the unhealthy instance with a new one.

- **Increases availability of application:** The Auto-scaling makes sure that the applications have the perfect amount of computing all the time automatically and provisions the capacity of the applications with Predictive Scaling.

- **Lowers the costs:** The Auto-scaling helps in adding up the instances when required and helps in optimizing the overall costs and performance by scaling across the various purchase options.

How does Auto-Scaling work?

The Auto-scaling works at different levels with different methods:

Fleet Management

No matter if you are using only a single instance EC2 or hundreds of it, you can opt for auto-scaling for detecting the impaired instances of EC2 along with the unhealthy applications. It also helps in replacing the unhealthy instances without any kind of manual intervention. This makes sure that the application is having all the capacity to compute that you require and expect. The Auto-scaling performs three major functions for automating the fleet management for the instances of Amazon EC2:

- It monitors the current health of all the instances which are running. It makes sure that the application of the user is in the state of receiving all the required traffic and that the instances of EC2 are working in the proper condition. The EC2 auto-scaling performs periodic health checks for identifying an unhealthy instance.

- It helps in replacing the impaired instances without any form of intervention. When an instance fails the health check, it is terminated and replaced by a new one by EC2 auto-scaling. Thus, you need not respond when there is any need for instance, replacement.

- EC2 auto scaling balances the capacity beyond various AZs. The auto-scaling system can naturally balance the instances of EC2 across different zones and launch the instances which are new, so it is possible to balance them between the various zones in an even manner.

Scheduled Scaling

It is always helpful when you can schedule a certain job as it automates the whole process and functions without manual intervention. The same thing is associated with scheduled scaling. It allows you to scale based on your required schedule and scale the applications much ahead of the known changes in load. For instance, every 7 days, the application traffic starts increasing on Monday, remains at the peak on Tuesday, and begins to decrease again on Wednesday. Therefore, with the help of scheduled scaling, you are able to easily plan your activities of scaling completely based on application traffic patterns known to you.

Dynamic Scaling

The auto-scaling EC2 feature enables the users to closely track the curve of demand for the applications, thus reducing the requirement for the manual provision of the capacity of EC2 beforehand. For instance, you can also use the policies of target scaling for selecting the required load metric, which is necessary for the application like utilization of CPU. You can also set the overall value of your target by using the feature of request count per metric target, which is available with an application load balancer, which is an option for the service of Elastic Load Balancing or ELB. EC2 auto scaling adjusts the number of EC2 instances automatically as required for maintaining the target.

Predictive Scaling

It is a feature provided by the service of auto-scaling that uses the technique of machine learning for scheduling the required amount of instances of EC2 within the prospect of the approaching changes in traffic of your application. With predictive scaling, you can easily predict the future application traffic that also includes the daily occurring spikes and sets up the right number of instances beforehand. The machine-learning algorithm of predictive scaling detects even the slightest changes in weekly or daily traffic patterns and adjusts the forecasts automatically. This, in turn, discards the requirement for adjusting the parameters of auto-scaling manually as the cycle changes with time.

CHAPTER 4:

Virtual Private Cloud (VPC)

Virtual private mists (VPCs) are anything. Still, difficult to utilize AWS arranges coordinators and incredible devices for sorting out your framework. Since it's so natural to separate the occasions in one VPC from whatever else you have running, you should make another VPC for every single one of your undertakings or venture stages. For instance, you may have one VPC for early application improvement, another for beta testing, and a third for the generation (see Figure 2.1).

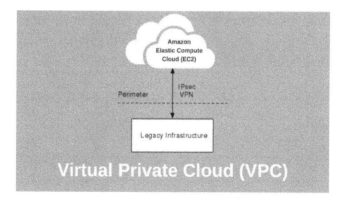

Tenancy

When propelling an EC2 example, you'll have the chance to pick a tenure model. The default setting is shared tenure, where your occasion will run as a virtual machine on a physical server that is simultaneously facilitating different examples. Those different cases likely could be claimed and worked by other AWS clients, although the plausibility of any sort of uncertain cooperation between examples is remote.

To meet uncommon administrative prerequisites, your association's cases may require an additional degree of disconnection. The Dedicated Instance choice guarantees that your occurrence will run without anyone else committed physical server. This implies it won't be imparting the server to assets claimed by an alternate client account. The Dedicated Host alternative enables you to recognize and control the physical server you've been appointed to meet progressively prohibitive authorizing or administrative prerequisites.

Normally, committed examples and devoted hosts will cost you more than occasions utilizing shared tenure. Exercise 2.1 will direct you through the dispatch of a basic EC2 Linux occurrence.

Choosing the right instance for your workload is essential to ensure the availability, scalability, and efficiency of your application. Amazon Web Services (AWS) offers several types of EC2 instances suitable for different sizes and purposes. But how to choose the best type of EC2 for your application? You need to know a little more about the subject to be able to choose more assertively.

T2, T3, M4, and M3: EC2 instances for conventional applications

For general purpose applications, these EC2 instances are the best choice, as they offer a balanced profile of computing, memory, and network resources.

T2 instances: recommended for medium-sized sites, web applications, and microservices.

T3 instances: update of T2 instances, with cost and performance advantages. They require minor changes to your configuration to work properly. They are also recommended for medium-sized sites, web applications, and microservices.

Configuring Instance Behavior

You can alternatively advise EC2 to execute directions on your occasion as it boots by highlighting client information in your case design (this is once in a while known as bootstrapping). Regardless of whether you determine the information during the support setup process or by utilizing the client information esteem with the AWS CLI, you can have content records carry your occurrence to any ideal state.

Client information can comprise of a couple of straightforward directions to introduce a web server and populate its Webroot, or it tends to be a modern content setting the occurrence up as a working hub inside a Puppet Enterprise–driven stage.

VPC Sizing and Structure

How to size VPC

A subnet is in an availability zone. Try to divide each subnet into levels (application, web, database, reservation). Since each region has at least three AZs, it is good practice to start dividing the network into four different AZs. This allows at least one subnet in each AZ and one reservation. Taking a /16 subnet and dividing it into 16 shapes will make each one a /20.

Custom VPC

The custom VPC is an isolated and resistant regional service. It works from all the AZ in that region and allows isolated networks within AWS. No IN or OUT of a VPC without explicit configuration. Isolated explosion radio. Any issues are limited to that VPC or anything related to it. The custom VPC has a flexible configuration with a hybrid network to allow connection to other cloud or local networks.

Default or dedicated location. This refers to the hardware configuration. The default settings allow one decision per resource. Dedicated locks any resources created in that VPC to be on dedicated hardware at an additional cost.

Custom VPC facts

Private IP and public IPv4

Assignment of 1 mandatory private IPv4 CIDR blocks

• Prefix min /28 (16 IP)

• Max /16 prefix (65,536 IP)

Can add secondary IPv4 blocks after creation.

• A maximum of 5 can be increased with a support ticket.

• When you think of VPC, you have a pool of private IPv4 addresses, and you can use public addresses when needed.

Single Assigned CIDR IPv6 /56 block

• Even in the maturing phase, not everything works the same way as IPv4.

• With the increasing use of IPv6, this should be added as default.

• AWS assigns the range since you have no choice about which range to use, or you can choose to use your own IPv6 addresses.

• IPv6 doesn't have private addresses; they are all addressed as public by default.

DNS provided by R53

Available at the base IP address of VPC + 2. If the VPC is 10.0.0.0, the DNS IP will be 10.0.0.2. Two options that manage how the DNS works in the VPC:

• Edit DNS hostnames

If true, public DNS hostnames are assigned to instances with public IPs in a VPC.

If false, this is not available.

• Edit DNS resolution

If true, the instances in the VPC can use the DNS IP address.

If false, this is not available.

VPC subnets

AZ Strong VPC subnet.

• If the Available zone fails, the subnet and services also fail.

• High availability requires multiple components in different AZs.

• One subnet can only have 1 AZ.

• 1 AZ can have zero or more subnets.

• CIDR IPv4 is a subset of the VID CIDR block.

• Impossible to overlap with other subnets in that VPC

• Optionally, the IPv6 CIDR block can be assigned to the subnet.

• (256/64 subnets can be adapted to /56 VPC)

• Subnets can interact with other subnets in the VPC by default.

Reserved IP addresses

There are five IP addresses within each VPC subnet that cannot be used. Whatever the size of the subnet, there are five fewer IP addresses than you expect.

• If you use 10.16.16.0/20 (10.16.16.0—10.16.31.255)

• Network address: 10.16.16.0

• Network + 1: 10.16.16.1—VPC router

• Red + 2: 10.16.16.2—Reserved for DNS

• Network + 3: 10.16.16.3—Reserved for future AWS use

• Transmission address: 10.16.31.255 (last IP in the subnet).

DHCP Option Set

This is how IT devices automatically receive IP addresses. There are several options applied simultaneously to a VPC and this configuration flows through the subnets. This can be changed, new ones can be created, but one cannot be changed. If you want to change the settings:

• You can create a new one

• Change VPC mapping to new

• Delete the old

IP allocation options

Automatically assign public IPv4 address

• This creates a public IP address in addition to your private subnet.

• This is necessary to make a subnet public.

Automatically assigns IPv6 address.

• For this to work, the subnet and the VPC need an address assignment.

VPC Routing and Internet Gateway

VPC Router is a high availability device available in every VPC that moves traffic from one place to another. The router has a network interface on each subnet of the VPC. Route traffic between subnets. Routing tables define what the VPC router will do with the traffic when the data leaves that subnet. A VPC is created with a primary route table. If a custom route table is not associated with a subnet, it uses the main route table of the VPC.

If you associate a custom route table created with a subnet, the main route table is decoupled. A subnet can only have one routing table at a time, but a routing table can be associated with many subnets.

Route tables

When traffic leaves the subnet with which this routing table is associated, the VPC router examines the IP packets for the destination address. Traffic will try to match the route to the route table. If multiple routes are found as a match, the prefix is then used as a priority. The higher the prefix, the more definite the route will be, therefore, the higher the priority. If the destination indicates local, it means that the destination is in the VPC itself. The local route can never be updated, they are always present and the local route always takes precedence. This is the objection to the prefix rule.

Internet portal

A managed service that permits gateway traffic between the Internet and the VPC or the AWS public area (S3, SQS, SNS, etc.). Regional resilient gateway connected to a VPC. An IGW will cover all AZs in a region used by the VPC. A VPC can have:

• An IGW

• No IGW and be completely private.

IGW can be created and connected to any VPC. It works within the AWS public area.

Using IGW

In this example, an EC2 instance has:

• Private IP address from 10.16.16.20

• Public address of 43,250.192.20

The public address is not public and is linked to the EC2 instance itself. Instead, IGW creates a record that links the instance's private IP to the public IP. That is why the private IP address is only displayed when creating an EC2 instance. This is important. For IPv4, it's not configured in the operating system with the public discourse.

Summary

The Virtual Private Cloud administration gives the systems administration establishment to EC2 and different AWS administrations. AWS abstracts some systems administration segments so that their arrangement is more straightforward than in a conventional system; however, despite everything, you have to have a firm handle of systems administration basics to engineer VPCs.

In every area, AWS consequently furnishes a default VPC with default subnets, a primary course table, a default security gathering, and a default NACL. Many utilize a default VPC for quite a while, never arranging a VPC without any preparation. This makes it even more significant that you as an AWS engineer, see how to put a virtual system foundation without any trial. There's a decent possibility you won't be permitted to adjust a framework that was based over a default VPC. Instead, you might be entrusted with duplicating it starting from the earliest stage—investigating different issues en route. Practice what you've realized in this section until making completely useful VPCs turns out to be natural to you.

In a conventional system, you're allowed to reconfigure server IP addresses, move them to various subnets, and even move them to different physical areas. You have the colossal adaptability to change your arrangements midstream.

Exercise

Allocate and use an elastic IP Address.

1. Allocate an Elastic IP address and associate it with the instance you created earlier.

2. Click Allocate New Address.

3. Click Allocate.

4. Click the EIP, and under the Actions menu, click Associate Address.

5. Select the instance you created earlier.

6. Click Associate. The instance original public IP address should change to the EIP.

CHAPTER 5:

Amazon Route 53

Route 53 and DNS

Amazon Route 53 is a system of scalable and available DNS or Domain Name System. You can use the services of Route 53 for performing three different types of functions and that too in any kind of combination: registration of your domain, health checking, and routing of DNS. If you want to use Route 53 for all the mentioned function, you need to follow these steps:

- **Register the names of the domain**

When you want to host a website of your own, the website needs a specific name, such as abcd.com. With Route 53, you can easily register the name for the web applications or website, which is known as the domain name.

- **Route the traffic to your domain resources**

When any user opens the browser and the name of your domain or the name of your subdomain in the designated address bar, Route 53 helps by connecting the browser with your selected web application or website.

- **Checking the health of the website resources**

Route 53 helps in checking the health of the resources. It does so by sending automatic requests to the resources over the internet, such as web server, for verifying it is readily available, reachable, and also functional. You can also select the option for receiving notifications when any of the resources becomes unreachable or unavailable and then choose to route away from the traffic from the unhealthy resources to a fresh one.

Registration of domain

You need a domain name while you create a web application or website for your content. Your domain name will look like abcd.com, which the users will be entering in the address bar for viewing the website. The registration of the domain name is an easy job.

- You need to start by choosing a domain and check, whether it is available or not. In case the domain name you want is already taken, you can try by choosing other words or by changing the domain like.com to another part like .hockey or .ninja. There are various top-level domains that you can find in the list of Route 53.

- After choosing the name of the domain, you need to register it using Route 53. While recording, you need to provide various information about the environment, such as the name of the owner and contact information of the owner of the field. When you register your domain with the help of Route 53, it will automatically make itself the service of DNS for that domain after performing the following:

1. Create a hosted zone that will have a similar name, just like the domain.

2. Assigns four name sets of the servers for the hosted zone.

3. Gets the name of the server's right from the hosted zone and will add them to your domain.

   - After the registration process, your information is sent to the domain registrar. The domain registrar can either Amazon Registrar Inc. or something else.

   - Your information will be sent out for the registry of the domain. A registry is nothing but the company, which sells registration for the domains.

   - The registry will be storing your domain information in the database.

In case you have already registered the domain name with any other registrar, the user can quickly transfer the same into Route 53. For this, it is not necessary to use the features of Route 53.

How is the traffic routed to a website using Route 53?

All the computers, smartphones, or laptop that serves content for the massive websites of retail, communicates with each other with the use of numbers. These numbers are known as IP addresses. The IP addresses are generally very long; however, when you visit a site, you do not need to remember the IP address.

You just need to enter the name of the domain, such as abcd.com. DNS services such as Route 53 helps in establishing a connection between the IP addresses and the terms of the parts.

Process of traffic routing

- When you enter a domain name and press enter, the domain name request is routed to DNS resolver, which is managed by the user's ISP.

- The resolver forwards the user request to the DNS root name server.

- The resolver again forwards the request for a domain to a TLD name server for the professions with .com. The name server then responds to the right of the user with four name servers of Route 53, which are associated with the domain. The resolver then caches the name servers of Route 53.

- The resolver chooses a name server of Route 53 and then forwards the request for the domain such as abcd.com to the name server.

- Route 53 looks into the hosted zone of abcd.com and gets the associated IP address for the webserver.

- The DNS resolver gets the IP address and returns the resulting webpage for abcd.com.

Hosted public areas

The hosted zone is a DNS database for a specific part of the global DNS data. The public hosted site is a type of R53 hosted zone hosted on public DNS name servers provided by R53. In the process of creating a hosted site, AWS delivers at least four DNS name servers that host the site. This is a globally resilient service due to multiple DNS servers. Hosted zones are automatically created when registering a domain with R53.

These Hosted zones can be created separately. If you want to register a domain somewhere else and use R53 to host the zone file and registrations for that domain, you can specifically design a hosted zone and point to an externally registered part in that zone. There is a monthly fee to accommodate each area housed within R53 and a commission for any questions asked of that service.

Hosted zones are what the DNS system refers to through proxy and name server records. A hosted zone, when referred to in this way by the DNS system, is known as authoritative for a domain. Become the only source of truth for an environment.

Route 53 health checks

Route checks will allow periodic integrity checks on servers. If one of the servers has an error, it will be removed from the list. If the error is corrected, the status check will be passed and the server will be added back to a healthy state.

Integrity checks are separate but are used by records within R53. Integrity checks are not created within the records themselves. These are done by a fleet of global health controllers. If you think they are robots and you block them, this could cause alarms.

By default, checks usually occur every 30 seconds. This can also be increased to 10 seconds for an extra cost. These checks are to verify status. Since there are many, you will get one automatically every few seconds. The 10-second alternative will complete multiple checks per second. There may be one of the three controls:

• TCP check: R53 tries to establish TCP with endpoints in 10 seconds.

• HTTP/HTTPS: same as TCP but in 4 seconds. The endpoint must respond with a 200 or 300 status code within 3 seconds of verification.

• String match: As above, the body must have a string within the first 5120 bytes. This is chosen by the user.

There are three types of controls:

• Endpoint checks

• Checks of checks

• CloudWatch alarms

Route 53 Examples of routing criteria include:

• **Simple:** direct traffic to a single resource. The client requests a resolution that has a record. It will respond with three values and these will be sent to the client. The customer then chooses one of the three at random. This is just a record. There are no health checks.

• **Failover:** Create two records with the same name and the same type. One is configured to be primary and the other is secondary. This is the same as a simple policy, except for the answer. Route 53 knows the health of both cases. As long as the primary is healthy, he will respond with this. If the health check fails with the primary, the backup will be returned. This is configured to implement passive-active failover.

• **Weighted:** Create multiple records with the same name within the hosted zone. For each of these records, a weighted value is provided. The total weight equals the weight of all forms with the same name. If all parts with the same name are intact, it will distribute the load by weight. If one of them fails its status check, it will skip it several times until a good one is hit. This can be used to migrate to separate servers.

• **Latency Based:** Multiple records can be created in a hosted area with the same name and type. When a customer request arrives, you know what region the right is coming from. He knows the lowest latency and will respond with the lowest latency.

• **Geolocation:** intended to provide results corresponding to the demand of its customers. The record will first be compared by country, if possible. If this does not happen, the registration will be verified by the continent. Finally, if nothing matches again, it will reply with the default answer. This can be used for license rights. If overlapping regions occur, the preference will always go to the smallest or most specific part. The United States will be chosen from the North American records.

• **Multi-value:** Simple records use a single name and multiple values in this record. These will be controlled by the state and unhealthy responses will be automatically removed. With various costs, you can have multiple forms with the same name, and each of these records can have a status check. The R53 using this method will respond to queries with each and every correct form but will remove any records marked as unhealthy from those responses. This eliminates the problem with a simple route where a single unhealthy record can reach your customers. A great alternative to simple routing when you need to improve reliability, and it's an alternative to failover when you have to respond to more than two registers, but you don't want the complexity or the overhead of weighted routing.

CHAPTER 6:

Amazon S3 and Cloudfront

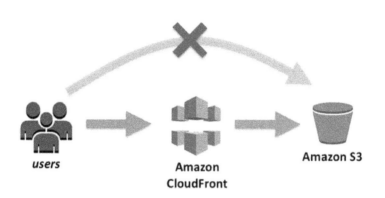

users   Amazon CloudFront   Amazon S3

1. What Is Amazon Simple Storage Service (S3)

Amazon S3 is an object-based storage service offered by AWS that is flexible, fast, and secure. Thousands of businesses and companies use S3 to store large amounts of data, applications, archives, etc. Among the established companies are:

⏹ Netflix:

Netflix is the world's top entertainment application to watch movies and TV shows. It uses S3 to store content before delivering it to a content delivery network.

⏹ Airbnb:

Airbnb is the top accommodation website that finds a place/hotel/resort for you to stay. No wonder, it makes use of S3 to store a massive amount of static files, data, and pictures and perform data analytics.

Many other renowned companies have access to S3. The reason being, it's convenient, easy to use, and most importantly, economical.

Basics of S3

Let's get down to the basics of S3. The S3 objects are used as web objects, which can be accessed through the HTTP/HTTPS protocol. Every web object has a unique URL in this format: http://bucket.amazonaws.com/key

If you've created an S3 item, it will be in the following format:

http://example.amazonaws.com/photos/ example-photo.jpg

Where the bucket name is "example" and the bucket points to the object name/key "example-photo.jpeg." Before you store data in S3, you must create a bucket. The bucket stores all the objects. When deciding the name of the bucket, there are a few rules you need to keep in mind:

⬜ The name must be unique and shouldn't overlap with other bucket names

⬜ Once you've created the bucket, you can't change the name.

⬜ The bucket name should be sensible and logical that exhibits the objects residing in the bucket because, in the URL, you'll see the bucket name followed by the object.

As for the region, you can choose any available geographical region where AWS stores buckets. The object can't leave the specified region, but it can be transferred to another area.

The key refers to the object name that acts as a unique identifier to find the data. It's the combination of a bucket, passport, and version ID that uniquely identifies the object. A resolution could either be an object name or can have a directory-like format such as folder/picture/random-photo.jpeg. Note that this format doesn't represent the structure of the AWS S3.

As for the region, you can choose any available geographical area where AWS stores buckets. In the example above, us-east1 refers to the part where the bucket is located. The object can't leave the specified region, but it can be transferred to another area.

The key refers to the object name that acts as a unique identifier to find the data. A resolution could either be an object name or can have a directory-like format such as folder/picture/random-photo.jpeg. Note that this format doesn't represent the structure of the AWS S3.

Amazon S3 Data Consistency Model

There are numerous data consistency models and Amazon S3 provides read after write consistency model, in which the object is read after it's created.

Let's take a simple scenario:

```
PUT  /photos/example-photo.jpg 500

GET  /photos/example-photo.jpg 500
```

The put and get commands are used to denote write and read, respectively. In this example, you write the object and read it that returns 500 response codes. Both of the commands run successfully.

Let's take another scenario:

```
PUT /photos/example-photo.jpg 500

PUT /photos/example-photo.jpg 500

GET /photos/example-photo.jpg 500
```

In this example, we are creating an object followed by another put request that overwrites the old objects' data, and then a "get" request is made to read the object and return output. In this case, we have an eventual consistency which means that the "get" request can return either the first put or the second put until the change propagates. The results may not be immediate but eventually, it will be visible.

Consider this last caveat scenario:

GET /hello-world.txt 404 not found

PUT /hello-world.txt 300 (Ok)

GET /hello-world.txt 404 not found

GET /hello-world.txt 300 (Ok)

We are making a get request for the object that doesn't exist. In this case, an error will encounter.

Then we make a PUT request and receive a 500 response code. The last command get is used, but we get an error "404 not found"

Why is that? AWS provides eventual consistency. It will recover the first resource and then the second.

If you use the get command again, you'll see that the object is successfully found.

Features of Amazon S3

Storage Classes

AWS offers a diversity of storage classes depending upon the usage and client's requirements. Each level provides a different purpose and is highly reliable that comes with a variable cost.

You chose a class that meets your use case scenario and requirements.

Amazon S3 Standard

Standard class is designed for users who want to access their data frequently. It has high storage costs and a low restore cost. If you've set access time as your priority, you can opt for a standard storage class. AWS sets the standard storage class as the default class if you don't specify the storage class of your own.

Reduced Redundancy Storage Class

The RR storage class is suitable for non-critical and reproducible data but it isn't reliable since data is prone to get lost and it's cheaper than standard class storage. If any object residing in RRS is lost, Amazon S3 returns an error.

The Intelligent Tiering Storage Class

This isn't a storage class, instead, it's responsible for moving the objects to and from storage classes depending upon how frequently the items are used. The main aim of this storage is to optimize storage charges by automating the mechanism of moving data to suitable storage without degrading the performance. You don't have to decide where and when you should move your objects because AWS continuously monitors your data and being the intelligent tiering class, it does the job for you. If the item hasn't been accessed for long, S3 will move it to an infrequent access storage class. However, if the object in the infrequent access storage is accessed more than once, it's moved back to frequent access storage.

Amazon S3 intelligently assess the access patterns of the objects and moves them when needed. No extra charges are deducted when objects are being moved between the two different storage classes. Note that the intelligent tiering type is recommended for object sizes greater than 128 KB. If the extent of the object is lesser, it won't be eligible for tiering.

Standard Infrequent Access Storage Class

The standard IA works best for storing data that doesn't have to be frequently accessed. It has the advantage of having longer storage time as compared to traditional storage.

Reliability and low delays ensure the safety of objects in the long run. The items remain in the storage for 30 days and the minimum size should be 128KB, otherwise, Amazon S3 will charge you if it's less than the recommended size.

It's particularly useful for storing backups, data, and disaster recovery files since they rarely require access, but should be accessed quickly at the time of usage. You can access the data in milliseconds (same as AWS standard storage class)

Amazon S3 One Zone Infrequent Access

Another service was introduced in April 2018 known as one zone infrequent access. It's relatively cheaper than standard IA because in one area IA, Amazon S3 stores the objects in only one availability zone which makes it less resilient as there can be a loss of data due to unreliability of the availability zone.

The storage cost is lower but it isn't as efficient as standard IA.

Storage Class for Archiving Objects

Amazon Glacier Storage Class

Amazon Glacier is designed for archiving data and has sufficient storage. You can either store high volume or low volumes of data, that too at a reasonable cost. Though, it takes hours to retrieve data that can put you at a disadvantage if you want to access the objects almost instantly. Unlike the S3 standard, Amazon glacier has meager storage costs and the objects have a duration of 90 days. If you want to access the data, there are various retrieval options such as expedite retrieval, standard, and bulk. You're charged according to the type of retrieval option you chose. If you want to access your data quickly, expedited retrieval allows you to do so in 1-5 minutes. When you've bulk of data, you can choose bulk recovery that lets you access your data in 6-12 hours. This type of storage has many uses such as storing archives of organizations, media resources, and backups.

Amazon Glacier Deep Archive Storage Class

In contrast to Amazon Glacier, the deep archive storage class is suitable for storing data that is infrequently accessed. The lifetime of data is approximately 180 days, which is greater than the time duration offered by other storage classes. By default, the retrieval time is 12 hours that may be a tradeoff but considering the cost of the deep archive, it's comparatively less expensive than Glacier. There is an option to choose bulk retrieval if you want to restore your data within 48 hours.

Reduced Redundancy Storage

As the name says, this Amazon S3 storage service allows users to store reproducible and uncritical forms of data. It's designed to sustain data loss by providing the option to store objects across multiple platforms, and giving 400x times the stability of a disk drive but makes sure that the redundancy is lesser than in standard Amazon S3 storage. It's backed by the Amazon S3 service level agreement. This is perfect for applications that require periodic replication of data such as any business application.

Get Started With Amazon S3

By now, you know that Amazon S3 is a powerful storage service that lets you store and retrieve data via the cloud whenever and wherever you are. We will use the AWS management console to get started. Let's get you a quick walk-through on how to set up Amazon S3.

Sign up

You need to have an AWS account to use Amazon S3. If you already have an account, head over to https://aws.amazon.com/s3/ and sign up for Amazon S3. You'll receive an email to notify you that your account is up and running.

Create a Bucket

You store objects in the bucket so first, you've to create a bucket. Note that you won't be charged for creating a bucket; you'll be only charged for storing and moving objects to and from the bucket.

Open the Amazon S3 Console and click on "Create bucket"

You'll find the bucket name field. Choose the name for the bucket. Make sure the name is unique from other existing bucket names in Amazon S3.

Chose the region of your choice where you want the bucket to be and then go to create. Congratulations you've successfully created a bucket!

How to Add an Object to a Bucket

Once you've created a bucket, you're all set to add an object. The object could be anything ranging from documents to media files.

Go to the **bucket name list** and click on the bucket that you wish to add your object to.

Go to **upload** and a dialog box will pop-up. Click on **add files** and choose the files you want to upload.

CHAPTER 7:

Amazon Block and File Storage

AWS service storage is a service that allows you to store data by transferring it over the Internet or another network to an offsite storage system managed by a third party, from personal storage for hosting or backing up someone's private mail, images, videos, and other confidential files, to professional storage that businesses use as a backup solution. The distance where they can securely transfer, store, and share data files. AWS service storage is an attractive cloud storage solution offered by Amazon to service providers to meet current data storage scenarios. With an AWS service AWS storage account, you can access two types of storage services:

Storage systems are generally expandable to suit the data storage needs of each individual or organization, accessible from any location, and versatile to allow any type of device to access it. There are three main models for businesses to choose from: a public cloud storage service for unstructured data, a private cloud storage service that can be protected with an enterprise firewall for more control over data, and a service hybrid cloud storage that combines public and private cloud services for increased flexibility.

Consolidate the Storage Infrastructure

The solution combines the best of two approaches with physical arrays for data center deployments and virtual arrays for smaller enterprise environments, such as remote sites or branch offices that require NAS (Network Attached Storage) storage.

- Automate data management

- Manage your data growth more efficiently.

- Improve IT agility and boost your business.

Accelerate business intelligence and decision-making with fast and innovative data movement between remote sites/subsidiaries/data centers and the cloud. The solution allows you to save administration hours and reduce costs by up to 60%.

Are There Any Hidden Costs In AWS Service Storage?

No, there are no hidden fees related to AWS service storage. However, in order to properly calculate the storage costs for your specific application, it is important to know what type of storage you want, whether it is Standard or Premium storage or managed or unmanaged disks.

The Scale of AWS service storage?

In terms of the scale required to bring applications closer to users around the world, Amazon covers more regions of the world than any other cloud provider.

AWS service storage Data Redundancy

Data redundancy and storage replication are very well supported in Amazon AWS to ensure that data is stored permanently and does not get lost. AWS service storage replication backs up data across multiple sites to protect it from any (natural) disaster, power outage, hardware failure, or any other planned or unplanned event. The four types of Amazon data redundancy are:

- Redundant local storage (LRS): the data is copied in triplicate in the same data center.

■ Redundant storage by zone (ZRS): the data is replicated synchronously on three storage clusters in the same region.

Being an excellent cloud service as it is, AWS service storage is constantly updated, extended, and innovated by the Amazon team. Recently, at Ignite, new products are to be presented and are briefly mentioned here because of their relevance for service providers.

AWS service storage types

Amazon Blob Storage:

■ Table Storage

■ Queue Storage

■ Disk Storage

■ File Storage.

Amazon offers a storage service within its cloud AWS offer. AWS service storage works on the principle of Amazon Blob (binary large object), data structures in which one can place any type of binary or text data. Amazon offers the storage of three types of Amazon Blob, depending on whether it is a block of data for large volumes of data.

Three redundancy levels are offered with an LRS mode (Locally Redundant Storage) with data replication restricted to a single geographic region, a grs mode (geographically redundant storage) with geographic image between two distant geographic areas, and finally a ra-grs mode.

The Amazon StorSimple option is a hybrid storage offer that combines cloud storage in AWS, with a storage array located on company premises. This solution is accessible to Amazon AWS customers whose annual bill exceeds 40 k € (approximately 62.5 TB of data hosted in AWS). In this case, Amazon installs a Xyratex 7020 storage array in the enterprise. This accelerates access to data stored locally but relies on AWS to extend the capacities of the bay thanks to the cloud. You can thus set up a geo-replication of local data to Amazon AWS data centers in Dublin or Amsterdam.

AWS Service Storage

- Capacity 3 types of storage offered: Amazon Blob objects of block type, Amazon Blob objects of page and disc type, and finally tables and queues. A file mode is in preview.

- Access management windows AWS active directory allows you to extend the company's active directory to AWS cloud services.

- Availability of interfaces of a REST API to access storage services.

- HDInsight (Hadoop cluster implementation) and StorSimple (hybrid hosting with a storage bay placed in the company and connected to AWS) options.

- Sla 99.99% guaranteed data access.

- Data location 15 datacenters in 5 global geographic regions, to choose from: United States, Europe (Dublin and Amsterdam), Asia/Pacific, Japan, Brazil.

- Amazon Blob in page mode (€ 0.038 per GB per month the first TB in LRS mode, € 0.071 in grs mode and € 0.09 in ra-grs mode), tables and queues (€ 0.053 per GB and per month the first TB in LRS mode, € 0.071 in grs mode and 0, € 09 in ra-grs mode).

Types of AWS storage account

AWS service storage offers several types of AWS storage accounts:

▪ Block Amazon Blob AWS storage accounts: Amazon Blob object AWS storage accounts only with premium performance characteristics.

▪ File AWS storage accounts: recommended for business or high-performance scaling applications.

▪ Amazon Blob AWS storage accounts: old Amazon Blob AWS storage accounts only.

Cloud storage is a special service today: it is inexpensive, saves a tremendous amount of capacity on computers and in data centers, and keeps you from having to add additional storage to your system. Amazon offers storage solutions for individuals and businesses, ranging from 5 GB of free cloud storage to 1 TB of cloud storage on one drive with an office365 (o365) account and almost infinitely scalable storage solutions.

Know more about the following and their importance:

- AWS blobs: massively scalable object memory for text and binary data.

- AWS queues: a messaging memory for reliable messaging between application components.

- AWS tables: NoSQL memory for storage without structured data schema.

An Intro to AWS Cloud Shell

The AWS cloud shell is a free bash shell, which you can run directly in the AWS portal. The AWS CLI interface is preinstalled and configured for use with your account. Click the cloud shell menu button located in the upper right corner of the AWS portal window:

You can also install and use AWS CLI locally.

An AWS service AWS storage account contains all of your AWS service storage data objects: Amazon Blob, files, queues, tables, and disks. The AWS storage account provides a unique namespace for your AWS service storage data, accessible from anywhere in the world via HTTP or HTTPS. The data in your AWS service AWS storage account is durable and highly available, secure, and massively scalable.

The AWS free account

The AWS free account like its name is totally free and you also get a credit of € 170 that you can use within 30 days. Once you've exhausted your free credit, you will be notified. So that you can choose whether or not to upgrade to a pay-as-you-go rate and remove the spending limit.

AWS service storage Amazon Blob stores large amounts of unstructured object data, such as text or binary data. Amazon Blob AWS service storage is highly scalable and available. Customers can access data objects in Amazon Blob Storage with power shell or AWS CLI, programmatically through AWS service storage client libraries.

The Amazon Blob Storage offers three types of resources which are:

▪ The AWS storage account.

▪ A container in the AWS storage account.

▪ An Amazon Blob in a container.

The AWS service storage service supports three types of Amazon Blob:

▪ The block Amazon Blob stores only text and binary data, up to about 4.7 tb...

▪ Add Amazon Blobs consist of blocks, like Block Amazon Blobs, but are optimized for add operations. Additionally, Amazon Blobs are great for scenarios such as logging data from virtual machines.

▪ Page Amazon Blob objects store random access files up to 8 TB in size. Page Amazon Blob Objects store virtual hard disk files and serve as disks for AWS virtual machines.

Move data to Amazon Blob Storage, several solutions exist to migrate existing data to Amazon Blob Storage:

AzCopy is an easy-to-use command-line tool for Windows and Linux that copies data to and from Amazon Blob Storage, between containers, or between AWS storage accounts. AWS data factory supports copying data to and from Amazon Blob Storage with an account key, shared access signature, service principal, or managed identities for AWS resources.

Amazon Blobfuse is a virtual file system driver for Amazon Blob AWS service storage. You can use Amazon Blobfuse to access your existing Block Amazon Blob data in your AWS storage account via the Linux file system.

Object Storage vs. Block Storage

In traditional IT environments, there are 2 types of storage, block storage, and file storage. These types exist with different providers such as AWS, open stack, and oracle. Block Storage operates the data at a low level, at a raw storage level, and manages the data as a group of numbered blocks.

File Storage operates at a higher level, at the operating system level, and handles data as a hierarchy of files and directories. This type of storage is intimately related to the one used by the operating system.

S3 object storage is a bit different. The storage is independent of a server is accessed through the internet. The data is managed by an API (Application Program Interface) over HTTP.

Each object contains data and metadata. They are held in buckets and have a key (filename) associated. Buckets are directories on which no more guides can be built, and can include an unlimited number of objects (files).

It is not possible to lie a bucket, open an object, install an operating system within S3, or run a database.

S3 is automatically replicated through multiple devices in multiple facilities within a region.

Similarly, the scalability, if the requests grow continuously, Amazon S3 will automatically partition the buckets to support many simultaneous submissions.

If traditional storage is required, AWS provides EBS, used by EC2. Also, EFS (Elastic File System) that provides storage that can be associated with multiple instances of EC2.

CHAPTER 8:

Amazon Storage Gateway

The AWS services of storage gateway allow seamless storage of hybrid nature between on-premises storage space and the cloud. It comes with efficient connectivity of the network to the services of cloud storage from Amazon. It delivers local performance at a virtually endless scale. The user can easily use it in their remote offices along with data centers for backup, archive, and restore, tired storage, and disaster recovery. The storage gateway connects directly to the local infrastructure as a virtual appliance and acts as a volume or also as VTL. The connection offered by storage gateway makes it easier for the organizations for augmenting the existing investments of on-premises storage along with high durability, high scalability, and low cost for a cloud storage solution. It is to be noted that the storage gateway does not function as an all-in-one solution for backup. The transfers and the backup are initiated by the existing host and are also managed by the same. It only acts as the portal for extending the infrastructure of data storage. This makes the storage gateway a flexible option as a portal. Storage gateway can be seamlessly integrated with various existing data storage configurations of an enterprise with no or minimal changes in hardware setup.

Gateway Types of Storage Gateway

Storage gateway comes with a variety of gateway types that can make your data transfer and backup a very easy and seamless process.

- **Join as a file server or File Gateway:** The interface of files allows the applications and on-premises servers' easy access as a network-sharing file to the storage gateway.

For boosting up the local performance of the servers, the data is cached. In Amazon S3, the information is also accessible as the objects in Amazon S3. For the protection of your S3 data with the help of native tools, you can use cross-region replication and versioning.

- **Connecting as local disk or Volume Gateway:** The storage gateway is presented by the volume interface to the application and on-premises servers as a local disk. The data available in these volumes is possible for transfer into the S3 cloud storage and can be accessed by the services of storage gateway. For the best performance, try to store the data locally along with backups in the cloud as a snapshot or blend upscale and latency by storing up the accessed data with the colder information locally in the cloud.

- **Connecting as a VTL or virtual tape library or Tape Gateway:** The types of equipment of tape automation along with the backup tapes are replaced by the tape interface with cloud storage and local disk. The existing recovery software and backup write up the native jobs of jam to the virtual tapes, which are stored in the storage gateway. You can easily migrate virtual tapes into S3 and archive the same into Amazon Glacier at a very low cost. The backup application helps in accessing the data and the visibility of all the backup tapes and jobs is maintained by the backup catalog.

- **Transferring data in and out of the cloud:** Storage gateway eases up your job of transferring data into cloud storage. It automatically cushions the data present in the on-premises server and moves it into the cloud storage. It also helps in moving out your data out of the cloud. This whole thing ultimately reduces the cost and time, which goes in transferring data between the AWS cloud and the site. Various optimizations are available such as delta transfers, multipart management, bandwidth scheduling, and bandwidth throttling, which are standard for all the available interfaces.

How to use the AWS storage gateway?

A storage gateway is generally installed on your host in the data center as a virtual machine. When the storage gateway is activated, the management console of AWS is used up for provisioning the storage volumes. The provisioned volumes can be mounted as iSCI devices on the on-premises servers. The importance, which is mounted, can be like any average storage volume by the local applications.

Critical features of storage gateway

- **Managed cache:** The appliances of the local gateway maintain the stock for the recently accessed or written data so that the applications can lower latency access to the data, which is stored in the AWS cloud. The storage gateway uses a write-back and read-through cache.

- **Standard protocols for storage:** The gateway of storage seamlessly connects with the local backup applications with SMB, NFS, iSCCI-VTL, or iSCSI. It helps in adopting the AWS cloud storage without any need to modify the applications. The device emulation and protocol conversion provided by the storage gateway enables the users to access the block data on the volumes, which are managed by the storage gateway.

- **Fast and optimized transfer of data:** The storage gateway helps in secure uploading of data and secure downloading of the data requested by the user encrypts any type of data that is in transit between any gateway appliance and AWS cloud by using SSL. Optimizations are applied for all the virtual and block tape data.

- **Integration of AWS:** Storage gateway is a native AWS service. It integrates with all other benefits of AWS required for backup, storage, and management. The storage gateway service stores the files as Amazon S3 objects, stores the EBS snapshots, which are generated by the volume gateway with EBS, and archives the virtual tapes in GLACIER. The service of storage gateway also integrates with the backup service of AWS for seamless management of recovery and backup of the volumes of volume gateway, helps in meeting the regulatory and business backup requirements, and simplifies the overall management of backup.

Adding to the features, storage gateway also provides a seamless experience of management by using AWS Console service for monitoring and security with the help of other services from AWS like CloudTrail, CloudWatch, IAM and KMS.

Summary

Amazon S3 provides reliable and highly available object-level storage for low-maintenance, high volume archive, and data storage. Objects are stored in buckets on a "flat" surface, but through the utilization of prefixes, it will be made to look like they're a part of a traditional filing system.

You can—and usually should—encrypt your S3 data using either AWS-provided or self-serve encryption keys. Encryption can happen when your data is at rest using either server-side or client-side encryption.

There are multiple storage classes within S3, hoping on varying degrees of information replication that allow you to balance durability, availability, and cost. Lifecycle management allows you to automate the transition of your data between classes until it's not needed and may be deleted.

You can control who and what gets access to your S3 buckets—and when—through legacy ACLs or through more powerful S3 bucket policies and IAM policies. Pre Signed URLs also are secure thanks to allowing temporary and limited access to your data.

You can reduce the dimensions and value of your requests against S3 and Glacier-based data by leveraging the SQL-like Select feature. You'll be able also to provide inexpensive and straightforward static websites through S3 buckets.

Amazon Glacier stores your data archives in vaults that may require hours to retrieve but that cost considerably but the S3 storage classes

Exercise

Calculate the Total Lifecycle Costs for your data

Use the AWS Simple Monthly Calculator (http://calculator.s3.amazonaws.com/index .html) to estimate the entire monthly costs of the scenario described at the start of this section. Even better, use a scenario that matches your own business. Attempt to include a full usage scenario, including requests, scans, and data retrieval. Note that you just access the S3 a part of the calculator by clicking the Amazon S3 tab on the left, and you'll be able to keep track of your itemized estimate using the Estimate of your Monthly Bill tab along the highest.

CHAPTER 9:

Amazon Elastic Container Service (ECS)

Virtualization Issues

Using the EC2 virtual machine with Nitro Hypervisor, 4 GB of RAM, and 40 GB of disk, the operating system can consume 60 to 70% of the disk and most of the available memory. Containers take advantage of the similarities of multiple guests operating systems by eliminating duplicate resources.

This allows applications to run in their isolated environments.

Image Anatomy

A Docker image consists of multiple layers and not a monolithic disk image.

Each row of a Docker image creates a new file system level on top of the previous one. Images are created from scratch or a basic image. Images contain read-only layers and images are layered in the embodiments.

The Docker container is the same as the Docker image, except it has an additional READ/WRITE level of the container. If you have many boxes with very similar basic structures, they will share the overlapping parts. The other layers are reused between the boxes.

Container Registration

Registration or container image center. The Docker file can create an image of the container where it is stored in the container registry.

The Docker hosts can also run several containers based on one or more embodiments.

A single image can spawn containers on many different Docker hosts.

Key Concepts of the Container

• Docker files are used in creating Docker images.

• The containers are portable and always work as expected.

• As long as there is a compatible host, it will run exactly as expected.

• Containers are lightweight, use the host operating system to lift heavy loads.

• File system levels are shared whenever possible.

• Containers run only the application and environment required for execution.

• The ports must be exposed to allow external access from the host and beyond.

• Application stacks can be multiple containers.

ECS—Container Service Concepts

• Accept the containers and instructions provided.

• ECS allows you to create a cluster (the cluster is where the containers come from).

• Container images will be found in a log.

• AWS provides ECR (Elastic Container Record)

• Dockerhub can also be used.

The container definition provides ECS with sufficient information about the individual container. A pointer to the image to be used and to the ports that will be exposed. Task definitions store resources used by the activity. This stores the task role, which is an IAM role that allows the task to access other AWS resources. However, the task itself is not highly available. So, the ECS service is configured by defining the service and represents the number of copies of a task that you want to scale and HA.

ECS Cluster Types

The ECS cluster manages:

• Planning and orchestration

• Cluster management

• Positioning motor

EC2 mode

The ECS cluster is created in a VPC. You benefit from the multiple AZs found within that VPC. You specify an initial size that will guide an automatic resizing group. ECS using EC2 mode isn't a serverless solution, so you need to worry about cluster capacity. The Container instances aren't delivered as a managed service; they are managed as regular EC2 instances. You can use spot prices or EC2 prepaid servers.

Fargate mode

This eliminates a significant portion of ECS administration overhead, which means no need to administer EC2. Fargate's shared infrastructure allows all clients to access the same pool of resources. The Fargate distribution still uses a cluster with a VPC in which AZs are specified. For ECS activities, they are injected into the VPC. Each activity is assigned a flexible network interface with an IP address within the VPC. They are then run as a VPC resource and you pay only for the help of the container you use.

EC2 vs. ECS (EC2) vs. Fargate

• If you are already using containers, use ECS.

• EC2 mode is useful for a high workload when the price is taken into account. This allows for spot and prepaid prices.

• Fargate is fantastic if you

  • Has a heavy workload but is aware of the overall costs.

  • Have small or explosive style workloads.

  • Use periodic or batch workloads.

CHAPTER 10:

Serverless and App Service

Evolution of Architecture

Monolithic

• It fails together.

• An error will bring down the entire system.

• Flakes together.

• Everything is expected to work on the same processing hardware.

• Accounts together.

• All components are always working and always charged.

• This is the least economical way to design systems.

Tiered

• Diverse components can be on the same server or on different servers.

• The components are paired because of the endpoints connected to each other.

• You can adjust the size of the server that runs each application tier.

• Use load balancers between tiers to add capacity.

• The levels are still tightly coupled.

• The levels wait for a response from each other. If one level fails, subsequent levels will also fail because they will not receive the correct answer.

• Rear loads on one level will affect the other groups and the customer experience.

• The stories must be operational and send responses even if they are not processing anything of value; otherwise, the system will not work.

Evolving With Queues

• Data is no longer moved between levels to be processed and instead uses a string.

• Often they are FIFO (first inbound, first outbound)

• The data is transferred to an S3 bucket.

• Detailed information is placed in the next space in the queue.

• The levels no longer wait for an answer.

• The load level sends an asynchronous message.

• The load level can add multiple messages to the queue.

• The queue will have an automatically scalable group to increase the processing capacity.

• The auto-scaling group will only make servers appear when needed.

• The queue has the position of the S3 bucket and passes it to the processing level.

Event-Driven Architecture

Event producers:

• Interact with clients or system monitoring components.

• It produces events in reaction to something.

• Events, errors, clicks, actions.

Event consumers:

• This is a piece of software waiting for events to occur.

• Measurements are taken and the system returns to standby mode.

• Services can be producers and consumers simultaneously.

• Resources do not wait to be used.

• The event router is required for the event-based architecture that also manages an event bus.

• It only consumes resources when organizing events.

AWS Lambda

Function as a service (FaaS)

The service accepts functions—event-driven invocation (execution) based on an event that occurred. The Lambda function is a code in a language.

Lambda functions use a runtime. It works in a runtime environment, a virtual environment ready to execute code in that language. Billing is done only for the duration of a function. There are no costs to have standby and ready-to-use lambda functions.

Lambda architecture

A certain amount of memory and an adequate amount of CPU is allocated to the runtime environment. The more memory is given, the higher the CPU you receive, and the higher the cost of the function to be invoked per second.

Lambda functions can be assigned an IAM function or an execution function. The runtime role is passed to the runtime environment. Every time that procedure is performed, the internal code has access to any authorization provided by the role authorization policy. Lambda can be manually invoked or controlled by events. Every time you invoke a lambda function, the equipped environment is new. Never store anything within the runtime environment; it's ephemeral.

Lambda functions, by default, are utilities and can access any website. By default, they can't access private VPC resources but can be configured to do so if necessary. Once configured, this allows access to resources only within a VPC. Except if you have configured your VPC to have all the necessary settings for public Internet access or access to AWS public space endpoints, Lambda cannot have access.

The Lambda runtime is stateless, so always use AWS services for output and input. Something like DynamoDB or S3. If an event invokes a Lambda, it gets the details of the event given to it at startup. Lambda functions can last up to 15 minutes. This is the upper limit.

Key considerations

• Currently, run a time limit of 15 minutes.

• Suppose each run gets a new runtime environment.

• Use the execution role that is taken when necessary.

• Always upload data from other services from public APIs or S3.

• Store data in other services (for example, S3).

• One million free requests and 400,000 GB of calculation seconds per month.

CloudWatch and EventBridge Events

It offers a near-real-time flow of system events that describes changes to AWS products and services. It is now encouraging migration to EB.

Critical concepts of CloudWatch events

• They can see if X happens to Y times, do Z.

• X is a compatible service that is the producer of an event.

• And it can be a certain period or period of time.

• Z is a compatible target service for event delivery.

The EventBridge is literally a CloudWatch Events V2 that uses the same underlying APIs and has the same architecture, but with additional functionality. Things created in one may be visible in the other.

Both systems have a default event bus for an AWS account. The bus is a stream of events that occur for any supported service within an AWS account. In CW Events, there's only one bus (implicit), it is not exposed. EventBridge may have additional event buses for its third-party applications and services. You can interact with them in the same way as the default bus.

In both services, rules are created, and these rule patterns correspond to the events that occur on the buses, and when they see a matching event, they deliver that event to a target. Alternatively, you can have schedule-based rules that correspond to a specific date and time ranges. The rules correspond to the next events or programs. The tradition matches an event and routes such event to one or more targets as defined in that rule.

Architecturally, the heart of the event bridge is the event bus of the default account. This is a stream of events created by supported services within the AWS account. Rules are generated and linked to either the default event bus or a specific event bus. Once the government completes the pattern matching, it runs and moves that event that has hit one or more targets. The possibilities are in themselves JSON structures and the data can be used by the destinations.

Gateway API (Application Programming Interface)

This is one way that applications or services can communicate with each other. The API Gateway is a service managed by AWS that provides AWS managed endpoints.

You can also authenticate yourself to show that you are the one claiming. You can build an API and present it to your clients for use. It allows you to create, publish, monitor, and protect APIs.

Turnover based on:

• Number of API calls

• Amount of data transferred.

• Additional features like caching

It serves as an entry point for serverless architecture. If you have local legacy services that use APIs, this can be integrated.

Change to a Completely Serverless Architecture With DynamoDB

Without server! This is not a thing, managing few or no servers. This aims to eliminate the overhead and risk as much as possible. The Apps are a collection of small, specialized functions that do one thing really well, and then stop. These functions are stateless and are performed in ephemeral environments. Every time they run, they get the data they need, do something, and optionally persistently archive the result in some way or deliver the product to something else.

In general, everything is event-driven. Nothing is running until requested. While not in use, there should be little or no cost. You should use managed services whenever possible. The goal is to consume as much as possible as a service, schedule as little as possible, and use the function as a service for any general-purpose computation needs, then use all those blocks together to create the application.

Example Without Server

• A user needs to upload videos to a website for transcoding.

• The user accesses a static website that runs the loader. JS is run directly from the web browser.

• The external authorization provider, in this case, Google, is authenticated by tokens.

AWS can't use tokens provided by third parties. The transcoder will obtain the location of the original S3 bucket video and use it for its workload. The output will be added to a new transcoding bucket and will insert an input into DynamoDB. The user can interact with another Lambda to extract the media from the transcoding bucket using the DynamoDB input.

CHAPTER 11:

Database

RDS—Relational Database Service

Database Refresher: This is the data storage and management systems.

Relational (SQL): SQL is the abbreviation of Structured Query Language, which is a feature of most RDS. The data structure is known as a schema.

• Defined in advance.

• Define the names of things.

• Valid values of things

• Types of data that are stored and where

• Correct the relationship between the tables.

This is defined before the data is entered into the database. Each row in a table must have a value for the primary key. There must be a stored value for each attribute in the table.

SQL systems are relational, therefore, generally define relationships between tables as well. This is defined with a join table. A join table has a compound key that is a two-part key. Keys composed together must be unique. The keys in different tables are ways to define the relationships between the tables. The schema and relationships of the table must be defined in advance, which can be difficult to do.

Non-relational (NoSQL)

It is not one thing, and it is a problem for everything else. Generally, there is no pattern or a weak one.

Key Values Database

This is a list of keys and value pairs. As long as each key is unique, no actual patterns or structures are needed. These are really fast and highly scalable. This is also used for caching.

Wide column file

DynamoDB is an example of a large column file database. Each row or element has one or more keys. A key is called a partition key. Keys other than the partition key are called the range or sort key are available. It can be a single key (partition key only) or a compound key (partition key and sort key).

Each element of a table can also have attributes, but they do not have to be the same between the values. The only requirement is that each element within the table must use the same key structure and must have a unique key.

Document

Documents are generally formatted with JSON or XML. This is the extension of a key-value store in which each document interacts through a unique ID for that document, but the value of the document content is exposed to the database that allows you to interact with it.

Suitable for orders or collection databases or to contact obsolete databases. It is also excellent for nested data elements within a document structure, such as user profiles.

Row Database (MySQL)

Often called the Online Transactional Processing Database (OLTP). If you need to read the price of an item, you must have that line first. If you want to see all the dimensions of each order, you must check each row. It is ideal for things dealing with lines and elements where they are constantly accessible, edited, and removed.

Column Database

Rather than storing data in rows on disk, they store it on a column basis. The data is the same, but it is grouped on the disk, according to the column, so each order value is stored together; each item, color, size, and product price are grouped. This is bad for 0 style processing but is great for reporting or when all values are required for a specific dimension.

Graph

The relationships between things are formally defined and stored in the database with the data. They are not calculated every time you run a query. These are great for relationship-based data. The Nodes are objects within a graphical database. They may have properties. Borders are relationships between nodes. They have an address.

Relationships themselves can also have attachments, so name pairs of values. It may want to store the start date of any employment relationship. It can store large numbers of complex relationships between data or between nodes in a database.

EC2 Database

It is a bad idea to do this. It splits an instance into multiple AZs, adds reliability consideration between AZ, and also adds a cost to move data between AZ.

Reasons why the EC2 database might make sense

• You must be logged in to the database operating system.

• You should ask yourself if a customer requests it, it is rarely necessary.

• Optimizing advanced database options (DBROOT)

• AWS offers options to optimize many of these parameters anyway.

• It may be a provider that requests it.

• DB or DB version not supplied by AWS.

• A specific version of an operating system and a database that AWS does not provide may be required.

Reasons why you really shouldn't be running EC2 database

• The administrator overhead is intense to manage the EC2 host.

• Disaster and backup management adds complexity.

• EC2 is running on an AZ. If the AZ fails, access to the database fails.

• We will miss the functionality of AWS DB products.

• EC2 is on or off; you cannot easily resize.

• Replication can be difficult to manage on its own.

• Performance is slower than other AWS options.

RDS—Relational Database Service

Basics:

• Database as a service (DBaaS)

• Managed database instance for one or more databases.

• There is no need to manage the hardware or the server itself.

• It manages engines like MySQL, PostgreSQL, Oracle, Microsoft SQL, and MariaDB.

• Amazon Aurora. This is very different from normal RDS; in fact, it is a separate product.

RDS Database Instance

It runs one of the few types of database engines and can contain multiple user-created databases. When you create a database instance, you access it using a database hostname, a CNAME, and this is resolved on the database instance.

RDS uses standard database engines so that you can access an instance of RDS using the same tools as if you were accessing a self-managed database. The database can be optimized to Memory db.m5 burst db.r5 general db.t3.

There is an associated dimension and a selected AZ. When you provision an instance, you provision the storage dedicated to that instance. This is the EBS storage space located in AZ itself. RDS is vulnerable to failure in that AZ. Memory can be assigned with SSD or magnetic.

io1: many consistent IOPS and gp2 with low latency: the same burst group architecture as in EC2, used by magnetic default; compatibility mainly for long-term historical uses. Billing is in hourly rate per instance for this computing. You will be charged for the allocated storage space.

RDS Multi-AZ (High Availability)

You can enable this option on the RDS instances. Secondary hardware is assigned within another AZ.

This is called a standby replica or a standby replica instance.

The standby replica has its file in the same AZ where it is located.

RDS allows synchronous replication from the primary instance to standby replication. Access RDS ONLY through the CNAME database.

CNAME will point to the main instance. Standby replication cannot be accessed for any reason through RDS. Standby replication cannot be used for additional capacity.

Synchronous replication means:

• Writes to the database occur.

• The primary database instance makes the changes.

• Simultaneously with writing, standby replication occurs.

• Standby replication confirms the writings.

If the primary database fails, AWS detects it and failovers within 60-120 seconds to switch to the new database.

This doesn't provide fault tolerance as there will be some impact during the change.

RDS Exam PowerUps

• Multi-AZ functionality is not a free tier, an additional infrastructure for standby mode.

• Generally, double the price.

• Standby replication cannot be accessed directly unless an error occurs.

• Failover is highly available, no fault-tolerant.

• Only in the same region (another AZ in the VPC).

• Backups are taken from standby to eliminate performance impacts.

• Failover can occur for several reasons.

• AZ Complete Disruption

• RDS primary error

• Manual failover for testing

• If you change the type of an RDS instance, it will fail to change that type.

RDS Backup and Restore

RPO: Recovery Point Objective

• Time elapsed between the last backup and when the error occurred.

• Amount of maximum data loss.

• It affects the technical solution and the costs.

• Companies often provide an RPO value.

RTO: recovery time objective

• The time between disaster recovery event and full recovery.

• It is influenced by processes, personnel, technology, and documentation.

RDS Backup

The first plug-in is the full copy of the data used on the RDS volume. Thereafter, the snapshots are incremental and only store the data change. When a snapshot occurs, there is a brief interruption in the flow of data between the computing resource and the storage. If you are using a single AZ, this may affect your application. If you are using Multi-AZ, the Snapshot happens on the standby replica.

Manual snapshots do not expire; you must clean them yourself. Automated snapshots can be configured to make things simple. In addition to the automatic backup, the transaction logs of the database every 5 minutes are kept in S3. Transaction logs store actual data that changes within a database to perform actual operations. This allows you to restore a database to a point in time, often with a granularity of 5 minutes. Automatic cleaning can last from 0 to 35 days. This means that it is possible to restore at any time in that time interval. This will use snapshots and translation logs. When you remove/delete the database, they can be kept but will expire based on the retention period. The only way to keep backups is to create a final snapshot that does not automatically expire.

RDS Backup Exam PowerUps

• The RDS creates a new RDS with a new endpoint address when performing a restore.

• When you restore a manual snapshot, you are setting it up at a single point in time. This affects the RPO value.

• Automatic backups are different; they allow a 5 minute time point.

• Backups are restored and transaction logs are played back to bring the database to the desired time.

• Restorations are not quick, think RTO.

RDS Reads Replicas

Kept in sync using asynchronous replication. First, write complete to the primary and standby instance. Once stored on disk, it is transferred to the replica. This means that there may be a slight delay. These can be generated in the same region or in another region. This is known as cross-region replication. AWS seamlessly manages all encryption, settings, and networks.

Summary

Amazon has invested several billion dollars to set up its AWS solution. This cloud computing solution allows any business to benefit from a set of its services (applications and software, secure storage space, hosting, data analysis, etc.).

And leave the maintenance to Amazon. Many tools that we use on a daily basis are based on the cloud and, in particular, the AWS cloud: Amazon Dynamics 365, Office 365, Power Bi, Cortana Intelligence, and IoT AWS. Every day, almost 2.5 quintillion bytes of data are created worldwide according to IBM. Data that must be hosted, forwarded, managed. To adapt, the AWS infrastructure continues to expand, and today, there are more than 50 Amazon data centers spread over your secure data in the AWS cloud

They are securely stored on servers. Restricted and privileged access, data encryption, protection of personal data... Amazon is the industry leader in establishing and respecting security standards.

Exercise

Create and Launch an Ami Based on an Existing Instance Storage volume

1. If necessary, launch an instance and make at least some token change to the root volume. This could be something as simple as typing touch test.txt on a Linux instance to create an empty file. Accessing Your EC2 Instance

2. Create an image from the instance's volume (you'll access the dialog through the Actions pull-down menu in the Instances Dashboard).

3. Launch an instance from the console and select the new AMI from the My AMIs tab.

4. Login to the instance and confirm that your previous change has persisted.

CHAPTER 12:

Amazon Aurora

A urora's architecture is VERY different from RDS. It uses a cluster that is a single primary instance or zero or more replicas. Replicas within Aurora can be used for readings during normal operation. It provides the benefits of Multi-AZ RDS and read replicas. Aurora does not use local storage for compute instances. An Aurora cluster possesses a shared cluster volume. It provides faster provisioning, improved availability, and best performance. The Aurora cluster works in different availability zones.

There is one main instance and multiple replicas. Applications read by applications can use replicas. There is a shared memory of up to 64 TiBs in all replicas. This uses six copies throughout AZ. All instances can access these storage nodes. This replication occurs at the file level. No additional resources are consumed during replication.

By default, the main instance is the only one that can write. The replicas will have read access. Aurora automatically detects hardware failures in shared memory. If an error occurs, immediately repair that area of the disk and recreate the data without damage. With Aurora, you can acquire up to 15 replicas, and each can be a failover destination. Failover will be faster because no memory changes are necessary.

• The shared cluster volume is based on SSD storage by default.

• It provides such high IOPS and low latency.

• There is no way to select magnetic storage.

• This is based on what is consumed.

• Billing with a high score or billed by the most used.

• The released memory can be reused.

If you reduce a large amount of storage space, you will need to create a new cluster and migrate the data from the old cluster to the new cluster. Storage is for the cluster and not for the instances, which means you can add and remove replicas without archiving, provisioning, or deleting.

Aurora endpoint

• Minimum endpoints

• The cluster endpoint always points to the main instance.

• This is used to read and write applications.

Reader endpoint

• It will point to the main instance if that's all there is.

• It will load the balance between all replicas available for reading operations.

• The additional replicas used for the readings will automatically balance based on the load.

Costs

• No free level option

• Aurora does not support micro instances

- Beyond RDS single AZ (micro), Aurora offers the best value.

- The calculation is billed per second with a minimum of 10 minutes.

- The file is billed with a lifetime watermark with GB-Month.

- Additional I/O cost per request made to the cluster shared storage.

- 100% DB size in backups is included for free.

- The 100GB cluster will have 100GB of backup space.

Aurora Restore, Clone, and Backtrack

Backups in Aurora work the same way as RDS. Restorations create a new cluster. The backtrack must be enabled for the cluster. This allows you to restore the database to an earlier time. This helps to corrupt the data. You can adjust the backspace of the window for which it will work.

Quick clones make a new database much faster than copying all the data. It refers to the original memory and writes only the differences between the two. It uses a small amount of memory and only stores data that has been changed in the clone or the original after cloning.

Aurora Serverless

Provides a version of the Aurora database product without managing resources. It still creates a cluster but uses ACU or Aurora Capacity Unit. For a cluster, a minimum and maximum ACU can be set based on the load and can even drop to 0 to pause. In this case, you will only be charged for the storage consumed.

- Billing is based on resources used per second.

- The same resistance of Aurora (6 copies in AZ).

ACUs are stateless and shared among many AWS clients and have no local storage.

They can be quickly assigned to the Aurora Serverless cluster when needed. Once ACUs have been assigned to a cluster, they have access to the cluster storage in the same way as a provisioned Aurora cluster.

There is a shared proxy fleet. When a client interacts with the data, it is actually communicating with the proxy fleet.

The proxy fleet streams an app with the ACU and ensures it can scale in and out without worrying about usage. AWS manages it on your behalf.

Aurora Serverless—Use Cases

• Rarely used applications.

• Low volume blog site.

• Pay only for resources while consuming per second.

• New applications with unpredictable workloads.

• Excellent for variable workloads like sales cycles. Can be expanded and reduced according to demand

• Good for database development and testing, you can resize it when not needed.

• Excellent for multi-tenant applications.

• Bill a user a dollar amount per month per license.

• If the incoming load is directly connected to multiple inputs, this makes sense.

Aurora Global Database

Presents the idea of secondary regions with up to 16 read-only replicas. Replication from the primary region to the secondary regions occurs at the memory level and typically occurs within one second.

• Excellent for cross-region disaster recovery and business continuity.

• Global reading scale

• Low latency performance improvements for international customers.

• The application can perform reading operations against reading replicas.

• There are ~ 1s or less replication between regions.

• It is a one-way replica.

• No additional CPU usage is required; this happens at the storage level.

• Secondary regions can have 16 replicas.

• Everything can be promoted to read or write in a DR situation.

• Maximum 5 secondary regions.

Aurora Multi-Master writes

This allows a cluster of Aurora to have multiple instances that can read and write.

• Single master mode

• One R/W and zero or more read-only replicas

• The cluster endpoint is normally used to write

• The read endpoint is used to balance the load.

Aurora Multi-master does not have an endpoint or load balancer. An application can connect to one or both instances within a multi-master cluster. When one of the R/W nodes gets a written request from the application, it instantly proposes that the data be committed to all file notes in that cluster. At this point, each node that forms a cluster confirms or rejects the proposed change. It will be denied if this conflicts with something that is already in flight. The write instance searches for a group of nodes to be agreed upon. If the group rejects it, it mistakenly cancels the write. Otherwise, it will replicate to all storage nodes in the cluster. This also ensures that the storage space is refreshed in the cache memory of other nodes. If a writer falls into a multi-master cluster, the application will move all future load to a new writer with little or no interruption.

DMS—Database migration service

A managed database migration service. It starts with a replication instance running on an EC2 instance. This replication instance performs one or more replication tasks. This is where the settings for database migration are defined. This is done using a replication instance. The origin and destination endpoints must be defined. These point to the physical and target databases. One of these endpoints must be on AWS. Full load migration is a unique process that transfers everything at once. This requires that the database be inactive during this process. This could take several days. Instead, Full Load + CDC allows you to perform a full load transfer and monitors any changes that occur during this period. Any changes acquired can be applied to the target. CDC migration is only valid if you have a provider solution that only changes need to be captured and works quickly. The SCT (Schema Conversion Tool) can perform conversions between types of databases.

CHAPTER 13:

Analytics

Elasticsearch

A mazon AWS Elasticsearch is a managed service for text search and document indexing. It is an open-source analytical engine using log analytics, real-time application monitoring, and clickstreams. The core services of Elasticsearch provide deployment and scaling of clusters (servers) for federated indexing and text search. The cluster is defined with various configuration settings, such as EBS volume, snapshots, redundancy, software version and VPC. There is support for instance stores and EBS volumes for data storage and attachment to a VPC.

Redshift

RedShift is well-suited to warehousing and analyzing petabytes of data to run SQL analytical tools. RedShift aims to provide a data warehouse solution using which tenants can run sophisticated SQL queries and business intelligence reporting tools in real-time and offline. RedShift analyzes behaviors, patterns, and trends for gaming, stocks, logs, twitters, sensor data, and clickstreams.

Elastic Map Reduce (EMR)

EMR enables tenants to run analytics on large data sets based on custom codes for various complex applications. Redshift, by contrast, is used for real-time and offline SQL queries and business intelligence analytical reporting tools only. RedShift data is structured, while EMR can run analytics on unstructured data.

There is an additional cost associated with EMR, so tenants typically do not run SQL queries with it.

More on Database...

'Read' Replicas

RDS enables horizontal scaling with 'read' replicas that allow you to scale out as database workloads increase elastically. Multiple 'read' requests are routed (split) among 'read' replicas to improve throughput and lower latency for average and peak traffic events. Adding 'read' replicas to an RDS-managed database would increase database capacity through a number of transactions per second. The effect of horizontal scaling is to distribute packets across multiple database instances. Read replicas are read-only copies that are synchronized with a source (master) database instance. There is support as well for locating 'read' replicas in a different AWS regions closer to customers or employees to minimize latency. Any 'read' replica can be promoted to a master for faster recovery in the event of a disaster. It is not an automatic failover, however, and is not the optimal solution for fault tolerance that is available with a Multi-AZ standby replica. Amazon AWS supports copying EBS snapshots between different regions. In addition, tenants can create 'read' replicas of an encrypted database to a different region. Any encrypted data remains encrypted while in transit, as well.

Amazon RDS for MySQL Multi-AZ Replication

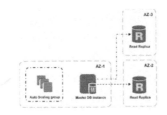

There is an RDS backup window that is configurable by tenants. It defines a time interval when AWS does a backup of the data. The backup window is configured by tenants when creating a database instance. AWS assigns a default 30-minute backup window at random if the tenant does not assign a backup window. In addition, there is a default backup window selected from an 8-hour block of time per region. RDS defaults the backup retention period to one day if configured using the RDS API or when the tenant does not configure the AWS CLI. The RDS keeps the default retention period to seven days if configured from an AWS console.

The source database is encrypted at rest and while in transit, for 'read' replications to slave databases within the cloud. Any 'read' replication requires selecting a target region and an encryption key for the target region. You can use your key or a default key generated by KVM in the target region.

The source database sends only read-only replica updates after the initial synchronization to the slave database(s). There currently supports up to five in-region and cross-region replicas supported per API call. In addition, Amazon permits a maximum of 40 RDS database instances.

Load Balancing

The native transparent load balancing is used to forward queries between all database instances assigned a unique DNS hostname, thus making them endpoints. Currently, there is no support for deploying ELB with Amazon RDS. The recommended solution for advanced load balancing is the AWS Application Load Balancer or HAProxy.

Database Migration Service (DMS)

Amazon AWS Database Migration Service (DMS) enables tenants to easily migrate from an on-premises SQL database to an Amazon AWS RDS-managed service. The service is initiated from Amazon DMS console where source and destination endpoints are configured to replicate database to the cloud. There are additional settings as well that determine how the database is replicated, including transformation rules, monitoring checks and logging. Identity and Access Management (IAM) security policies are configured by tenants based on their requirements. They are typically similar permissions and roles to the rules of when the database was originally on-premises at the enterprise data center.

RDS Storage Types

The storage and database instance types provide vertical scaling of capacity when initiating Amazon RDS services for an application. Tenants can specify the data storage type and provide a storage size (in GB) when creating or modifying a database instance. The storage type assigned to your instance is changed as well, by modifying the database instance. The options are provisioned IOPS, general-purpose (SSD) or standard (magnetic). There is a fixed amount of IOPS assigned to general purpose and magnetic storage types based on storage size. A provisioned IOPS enables allocating an amount of dedicated IOPS (input/output operations per second) to a database instance. A magnetic storage type is still available for backward compatibility; however, it is not recommended for new deployments.

An immediate outage occurs when converting to a different storage type, and data for that database instance is migrated to a new volume. Increasing the allocated storage, however, does not cause any outage. The database instances are assigned to an instance class (type) as well. The attributes include standard vCPU, memory and network throughput limits. In addition, some instance types are EBS-optimized and IOPS-optimized for maximum performance. Instances with EBS-optimized volumes do not share network bandwidth with other traffic.

Amazon RDS recently increased the maximum database storage size up to 16 TB when using provisioned IOPS and general-purpose (SSD) storage. Standard redundancy features include multiple availability zones (Multi-AZ) and 'read' replication for scalability.

RDS creates a database instance with multiple database tables, with assigned processing and volume disk size. The advantage of a larger database size and a higher IOPS is higher workloads on a single Amazon RDS instance, without distributing the data across multiple instances.

RDS Use Cases

Example 1:

RDS is preferred for an online transaction processing application (OLTP) where there are significant workloads. The storage type recommended for transaction processing applications with I/O-intensive workloads is the provisioned IOPS. The IOPS rate and storage space allocation are selected from a tenant range when the database instance is created. In addition, you can allocate additional storage and convert to a different storage type at any time.

The database instance type used with database instances specifies capacity with the number of IOPS and the network throughput (in Mbps). Amazon recommends a subset of instance types (M4, M3, R4, R3, and M2) optimized for IOPS storage when the database uses a provisioned IOPS storage type. General-purpose (SSD) storage type is typically used for small to medium-sized databases with moderate workloads and IOPS throughput requirements.

Example 2:

You have enabled Amazon RDS database services in VPC1 for an application with public web servers in VPC2. How do you connect the web servers to the RDS database instance so they can communicate, considering the VPCs are in different regions?

Any traffic sent between EC2 instances and AWS services in different regions (cross-region) must traverse the internet. Each VPC must have an Internet gateway in a public subnet and a default route in the Internet gateway's custom route table. EC2 instances, for the web servers and the RDS database instance, are assigned to a public subnet associated with a custom route table within each VPC. In addition, EC2 instances and database instance(s) are assigned an elastic IP (EIP) addresses for internet access. It is preferable to use EIP instead of public IPv4 addresses for persistence. The database instance in VPC1 must allow public access. RDS automatically creates a public subnet for your database instance when selecting the VPC option to create a new VPC and a public-accessible option and changing it to 'Yes.'

RDS for Microsoft SQL Server

RDS-managed service support from Microsoft SQL Server database mirroring and vertical scaling. The primary database of Microsoft SQL Server mirrors real-time data to a standby replication server for fault tolerance. Database requests are redirected to the standby server for failover only when the primary is not available. As a result, only the warm standby service is available with the SQL server for disaster recovery.

Amazon supports backup/restore of the SQL server database instances to S3 storage as well. RDS provides vertical scaling of SQL database instances to increase capacity. Tenants can increase allocated storage to the database instance and assign a larger instance type.

RDS for MySQL

There is support for real-time database replication with RDS for MySQL database instances and Multi-AZ failovers. The master and standby replicas are assigned to different availability zones. The primary database server replicates data in real-time to standby replicas. That allows the tenant to send 'read' requests to the primary and replica database instances. That feature is not available with Microsoft SQL Server for RDS. Also, RDS manages failovers to the replica during an outage. Database requests are redirected to the standby replica when the primary database is not available.

CHAPTER 14:

Application Integration

What is the Amazon Simple Queue Service?

Amazon SQS is a messaging service introduced by Amazon to administer asynchronous communication between applications or services.

The term "Queuing" in Amazon Simple Queue Service may be confusing to most of you. Take an example of communication between two subscribers via a cellular network. There are two speakers: The sender who sends the message and the recipient who receives the message. If there is direct communication between the two, both users need to be active.

Asynchronous communication is related to the messaging service, however, the main underlying difference is if the recipient is offline at the moment, the message sent by the sender will be on hold in the server. As soon as the receiver is available, the message will be delivered and received by the recipient.

Messages are processed in two ways:

Standard queues: It'sThe default type can handle multiple messages in any order in the line. It makes sure that the message is delivered at least once, and the duplicates are sent into the line.

FIFO queues: It offers first in first out the delivery. The order of the messages is preserved, and the message is delivered only once. The news is available to the receiver unless he/she deletes it.

How does Amazon SQS work?

Message Lifecycle

1.   The producer sends a message to a queue, and the message becomes redundant as it spreads across the Amazon SQS servers.

2.   When the recipient is available to receive the message, it consumes the news present in the queue, and the message is returned. As the message is being processed, it remains in the line throughout the visibility period. The visibility timeout is the time frame when the transmission is secure from receiving and processing by other recipients.

3.   The receiver deletes the message from the queue to stop the message from being received and going through the same process again when the time out clock expires.

Benefits of using SQS

The use of Amazon SQS has proven to be beneficial.

1.   Easy setup

SQS is a managed service for which you don't have to set up the infrastructure. All you've to do is simply use the API to read and write messages.

2.   Multiple Options

You can either chose the Standard queue or FIFO queue depending upon your requirements.

3.   Pricing

When you're using Amazon SQS, you only pay for what you use.

4.   Remove duplication

FIFO queues make sure there aren't any duplicate messages. This makes it suitable for tasks that require each task to be done only once.

5.   Checks for processing issues

If a message isn't processed, it is sent to the dead-letter queue where you can monitor it.

Cons of Amazon SQS

1.   Doesn't support broadcasting

Amazon SQS doesn't allow multiple entities to access the same message, making SQS not so suitable for one to many broadcasts. However, you can use an additional service called SNS along with SQS to enable broadcasting.

2.   High cost

Although you only have to pay for what you use, if the number of messages you send increases, it will add up to your bill. When thousands of messages are being processed every day, the cost of using the SQS system becomes higher, which is an overhead.

Use cases of Amazon SQS

Amazon SQS can be used in conjunction with other Amazon services such as Amazon EC2, Lambda and Amazon S3. Aside from that, you can use it to send tasks between different components of the system.

Amazon SQS can be used for scheduling batch jobs as it can maintain a queue of all the scheduled jobs so you don't have to track the job status. SQS takes care of handling the system.

Moreover, the service is effective for large distributed workloads where it's important to maintain queues of all tasks needed to be processed and distributed.

What is the Amazon Simple Workflow Service (SWS)?

Amazon SWF allows you to develop distributed applications by providing a programming model that lets you coordinate work across distributed components.

The central concept in Amazon SWF is the workflow.

A workflow is a group of activities that have some objective and logic to coordinate the activities.

For example, a workflow could be that it receives the customer order, and actions will be performed to process the order.

Terminologies

Workflow: A group of activities that have objective along with logic to coordinate the activities.

Workflow history: It stores information about the workflow execution/instance. The record includes which activities are being scheduled, their status, and results.

Domain: Workflow runs in an AWS resource called a domain. An AWS account can have multiple accounts having multiple workflows.

Activities: A task to be performed. It's registered with SWF as an activity type and information such as name, version, and timeout.

Activity Worker: It's a program that receives the tasks, performs actions, and outputs the results. An activity worker could be either a person or a program.

How does Amazon SWF work?

Some activities may need to be carried out more than once. For instance, in a customer order workflow, the customer can buy more than one item, and so the activity would run multiple times. This is denoted by an activity task that refers to one invocation of an activity. An activity worker that receives activity tasks processes it and outputs a result. The task can be performed either by a user using an activity worker software or by the application itself. The activity tasks are run synchronously or asynchronously. They are distributed amongst multiple networks spread across different regions. They can be written in any high-level programming language and run on any OS. The logic in a workflow is found in a software program called a decider. The decider's main purpose is to schedule activity tasks, provide input to the activity workers, and process the events.

What is Amazon Simple Notification Service?

SNS supports various terms, such as http, SQS, and email. It gives the sender the view, for example, as a single device type and platform sent to all. Amazon SNS uses a publish / subscribe model for message delivery. Subscribers are also known to recipients who subscribe to any topic of interest. Senders (publisher) send a message to a case, which in turn is delivered to all recipients who have subscribed to the topic.

Terminologies

Topics: Topics could include events, access point, or application that has content. Each topic includes a URL that locates the SNS endpoint.

Subscribers: Subscribers could be end-users, clients, servers or devices that can receive notifications of any topic.

Owners: Owners have the authority to create topics and have access control.

Publishers: Publishers send messages to topics. SNS matches the case against the subscribers who are found to be interested in the case and the message is delivered to every subscriber.

Amazon SNS API

You can use the SNS API to perform various functions:

1.   CreateTopic: This function lets you create a new topic. The topic name can contain upper and lower case characters, numeric digits and should be up to 256 characters long.

2.   AddPermission: This function sets up publishers and subscribers having access to the topic.

3.   Subscribe: The subscribe function includes the information of the subscribers interested in a particular topic.

4.   ConfirmSubscription: This function allows you to send a confirmation message to the end-user. The subscriber would confirm it by clicking on the link attached in an email.

Use Cases

   System Alerts:

System or application alerts are notifications generated when any event occurs, such as a change in the system. The notification is sent to the end-users.

   Push email and SMS:

There are two ways through which messages could be transmitted - email and SMS. Amazon SNS is used to target the audience/subscriber through email or text message. The interested audience could then decide to choose whether they want to visit the website or not.

Mobile Push Notifications

Amazon SNS is also used for mobile push notifications in which the message is sent to any mobile app by SNS. The notification could be in the form of an update, a newly added feature, and others.

CHAPTER 15:

AWS Certification Exam Taking Strategy

L et's look at a strategy that is effective for the SAA-C02 level examination. When you're taking the exam, the process is to take the exam in about three passes. The first step is to choose what you know and go with the answers you feel confident. And if you aren't secure, let's say you are spending five to seven seconds on one question, and you're not sure it could be option A or B, then mark that question and move forward. Don't spend much time on any problem in your first pass. So the first step is to move with confidence, picking the one you know, and then you will be able to check it at the end of the exam. And always go back and review all the answers from the start.

Next is the second step when you use the elimination process. You begin by analyzing the answers available, and looking at those options you know are incorrect and eliminate those that are wrong. It could be written in such a way to confuse you, but you know well that Amazon S3 does not work in that way, or with VPC, it is just not possible, so this is the elimination process. Using this method, the answers are limited to only a few options, and one can be right.

And the third step is just to review. Search the whole exam to find the marked questions and spend more time on them. So check the items many times that you have left, and then you have enough time to think carefully about these questions. So try not to spend too much time on one item; please remember the first step, and just continue. So you've got the first pass, the second pass, then the third pass where you'd like to search the exam and answer all the remaining questions.

And now that you are done and pretty confident, so if you have time left, you should review the questions repeatedly because you want to ensure that these answers are right. Even if you're not entirely sure of one or two questions and still don't know what the answer is precisely, maybe it's 100 percent right, so you should be happy that you have done your best. You have spent all of your knowledge, and if you have gone through all those three passes and you feel pretty good about it, then you have done a great job.

If you are inherent with the knowledge, skills, and abilities, just do your very best. When you panic, you will respond incorrectly, even if you know the answers. So you should answer all the questions in the examination to the best of your ability. This strategy works with many people, so remember these three passes when you take the examination and go back to your questions to ensure that you do your best to pass the SAA level exam.

Conclusion

Thank you for making it to the end. We cannot tell you that you could pass this exam. Instead, in this e-book, we try to describe the various resources available to you if you are a member of Cloud Academy. Finally, we give you some tips from the cloud community that we hope you have an idea for this test. This book will provide you with a good sense of AWS performance, best security practices, underwriting, and compliance storage capabilities.

Therefore, you need to know more about the basics of the service to pass exams. You should also be familiar with scenarios in which a particular service may be used. Therefore, you should consider these architectures and try to understand them as much as possible.

Based on the information above, we can conclude that there is a huge need for AWS certification and that the human resources available for this type of skill are insufficient. Therefore, it's better to learn these skills now than to compete the next time

With the rapid expansion of digitization and the IoT (thanks in particular to the smartphone industry), the area of cloud consumption is truly huge. Big enough to withstand its competitors. Since it depends on the consumer, you prefer at least one trial on AWS, which appears to be attractive enough to be accepted by consumers forever. Today's long-tail use case could reach the size of the entire cloud computing market in 2017 in the next 10-12 years—Google, Digital Ocean, and Microsoft are well-positioned to take advantage of Amazon's offerings. However, in terms of "time required," AWS has a better advantage over these competitors.

With the growing wings, in which AWS Nokia has already shaken hands for 5G, IoT, and cloud services, it has attracted the attention and confidence of cloud customers/service providers. Due to the seriousness of the results, employees are ready to work with AWS. In addition to the goodwill rights, AWS can also meet modern cloud service requirements. It provides its clients with access to a full set of virtual computers at any time via the Internet. For this reason, AWS Cloud Services, with its double error, will overshadow its peers and extend its approach over time.

In practice, a company will only need more than one server if it has users who cannot host it. Given the cost savings, we could also consider maximizing profit margins, and here AWS will play an important role.

Given the increasing enlightenment of cloud computing and associated costs, companies will naturally reduce their prices to face competition, but for what purpose? You also need to maintain the brand value (as before). They also offer services offered by AWS at relatively higher prices. In this case, the consumer will ultimately benefit from the limited competition and the search for a dominant position. Prices will be so low that cloud services will be cheaper than Internet connections. If the infrastructure were not as high as the demand we see today, consumers themselves would face a crisis.

I hope you have learned something!

CPSIA information can be obtained
at www.ICGtesting.com
Printed in the USA
BVHW040412201120
593625BV00025B/1566